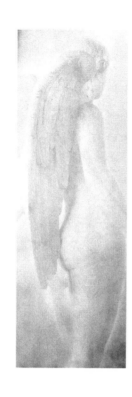

WHEN EVERY DAY MATTERS

A Mother's Memoir
on
Love, Loss and Life

Mary Jane Hurley Brant

THE SIMPLE ABUNDANCE PRESS

Published by
 Simple Abundance Press
P.O. Box 77420
Washington, DC 20013
www.simpleabundancepress.net

Isbn- 978-0-9817809-0-0
Isbn- 0-9817809-0-3

For my precious grandchildren
Connor Thomas, Ella Catherine and Gracen Jane

Table of Contents

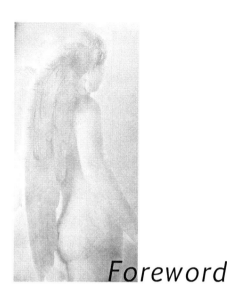

Foreword

On the following pages you're going to meet two very good friends of mine—a dynamic mother and daughter duo—Katie and M.J. Brant. Their story and my cherished friendship with both of them, through the very mystical chain of chance and connection we call Real Life, has been a tremendous blessing and it gives me deep joy to be able to share them with you.

I met Katie first, in the autumn of 1996. The only way I can describe her is as beautiful and bubbly as the finest champagne. Katie was one of those extraordinary women who grab you at hello with their charm, wit, grace and moxie. For within the space of a few dazzling minutes she revealed quite matter-of-factly that she had a malignant brain tumor and that the cancer had been diagnosed during her freshman year at college. Katie was then 25 and on a mission.

It didn't take long to realize that Katie had lived through more in her short life than many of us experience in a lifetime, but it was clear there was no room in her world for pity, only friendship, dedication and purpose. Katie had a clear vision of what she wanted to accomplish in her life which was the expansion of cause-related marketing, where successful corporations donate a portion of their earnings to non-profit organizations. Of course today cause-marketing is considered standard in corporate America but back then it was a lofty dream. In a very real sense, Katie Brant was one of cause marketing's pioneers. Her gentle but passionate perseverance and unflinching belief that we could convince the corporate world to look beyond the bottom line was the spiritual catalyst for many projects supported by The Simple Abundance Charitable Fund.

In the short time that I knew her, Katie accomplished so much! Like her family and friends, I watched in awe and admiration as she designed a pilot project in Cause-Related Marketing for Time Warner, Inc, then became the National Director for Corporate Marketing at UNICEF, and finally established her own foundation, Katie's Kids for the Cure dedicated to funding medical research into the cause of pediatric brain tumors, the leading cause of cancer death in children under 15.

As a parent, the wounding we fear the most is the death of

a child. It is the nightmare you pray will never befall you, if you can even bring yourself to articulate that prayer. It is the phone call you pretend you'll never receive. It is the unthinkable. But the unthinkable happens every day to women somewhere and on July 10, 1999, it happened to Mary Jane Brant.

When the unthinkable is reported in the newspaper, you can turn the page. On the six o'clock news? Turn it off. But when the unthinkable happens to someone you know, you're forced to think, and then you become terrified. Women whose children have died often feel betrayed by other women; it seems as if we avoid them (sometimes we do) and even stop mentioning their dead child. (We're silenced by guilt and unnameable fear). It's not that we're like Job's friends, who concluded that he brought his misery on himself. We're the friends of Job's wife. The Bible doesn't tell us what they said, but I'd be willing to bet it wasn't what was said that mattered, it was what they thought. *If it can happen to you, a woman who is so good, kind and loving, what can happen to me and mine?*

In her moving meditation on what matters most in life, *When Every Day Matters,* M.J. Hurley Brant confronts the unthinkable with courage, compassion and candor. If we are alive, we cannot escape loss. Loss is part of real life. When reading her exquisite evocation of life after loss, I am reminded of a story about a woman whose only child died and was bereft, inconsolable and alone. She went to the Buddha to ask his help in healing her wounded spirit. If he couldn't she would follow her child to the grave and forgo her destiny, karma be damned. She would not, could not continue to live this way. The Buddha agreed to help but told the mother she must first bring him back a mustard seed from a house that had never known sorrow.

And so the woman set out to find one. Her search took her a long time. She went from house to house all over the world, but there was not one that had never entertained grief as a guest. However, because every house knew what her pain felt like, they wanted to give her a gift to ease her anguish. It could not make it go away, but it might help. When the woman returned home she opened her heart and showed the Buddha what she had been given: acceptance, forbearance, understanding, gratitude, courage, compassion, hope, truth, empathy, remembrance, strength, tenderness, wisdom and love. "These gifts were given to help me," she told him.

"Ah, they were? And how do you feel now?" he asked the woman.

"Different. Heavier. Each gift comforts me in its own way, but there were so many I had to enlarge my heart to carry them all and they make me feel sated. What is this strange full feeling?"

"Sorrow."

"You mean I'm like the others now?"

"Yes," said the Buddha softly. "You are no longer alone."

It is my prayer that you, dear Reader, will be blessed by the authentic gifts of *When Every Day Matters* in a way that brings comfort between and beyond the lines and what's more, you won't feel alone.

Sarah Ban Breathnach

April, 2008

Introduction

In my End is my Beginning.

~MARY STUART, QUEEN OF SCOTS~
1542-1587

The life that I knew, the life that I had dearly loved died when my daughter Katie died. Today is the start of another. Katie was not only my daughter, she was my hero. This narrative is about her. I invite you to get to know Katie; I invite you to get to know me. Katie died of a brain tumor. When she left my world and this world at age twenty-eight, the reality of her absence created a space and chasm so deep within me that I felt like I was dying too; then I wished that I could. I felt unable to reconcile the moments of her death with the moments of her life; the moments of my personal despair with any moments of hope. And, as Shakespeare said in King John, "Grief fills up the room of my absent child."

Feeling completely fatigued and distressed and in need to reevaluate everything in my life, I called my sister-in-law Wendy and asked, "What will I do without Katie?" Her response was immediate.

"You will write and paint and sculpt." Later that day, I asked my ever supportive friend Lennie the same question. "I don't know for certain, but you'll need to continue your private counseling practice and maybe you'll write that book you've always talked about." My sweet cousin Irene told me the same thing. Still not convinced, I called my dear writer friend Sarah Ban Breathnach. She asked me, "How are you managing, M.J.?" That was when I started crying; I told her I had begun writing and keeping a journal. "Dearest M.J., you must write yourself back to sanity, serenity, and wholeness." Indeed, these women validated my personal belief system that says tell a wise woman your truth or tell no one at all. I took their combined advice; traveled the labyrinth down into my heart and turned my journal into letters to Katie. These letters cover the initial year following my beloved daughter's death. They were my journey back to life.

This book is a memoir full of factual information about Katie, my inner and outer life, and our family's life. I've added some psychological interpretations and insights that nod at my professional life as a psychotherapist. The dates above the salutation, "Dear Katie," reflect the approximate date of entry during that first grief stricken year. The tone of my letters is reflective and conversational because I won't allow death to cut off my communion with her, not now, not ever. I also don't just write about Katie's illness and death, dear Reader, because I don't believe those topics define a person - his or her life does. I hope as you read you will discover that the stretch marks which gave life to this story are not just on my body, they are on my soul.

M. J.

When you really want to pray for something and you do not receive it, you tend to believe that your prayer was not answered.... it is true that at times your prayer is not answered in a direct way.... Unknown to you, that prayer has secretly worked on another aspect of the situation and effected a transfiguration which may become visible only at a later stage.

~ JOHN O'DONOHUE ~
ETERNAL ECHOES

July 14, 1999
Dear Katie,

Today you have been gone four days. There is no part on my body that does not hurt. I am overwhelmed with missing you and the thought of what lies ahead. I feel like no one will ever know how I feel about losing you, my sweet and precious Katie. Can you see me now? Are you safe now? Where are you, Katie? Where did you really go? If I could only know the answers to those questions I might be able to survive.

We hoped that this day would never ever come, Katie. But it did come and now you are gone. We are no longer together in this world. It is final and I will never see you again. This thought fractures me. People said your funeral Mass was beautiful. Was it? I only know that you are not here. I don't care about the Mass or anything really. I don't care if I wake up tomorrow. For what is here for me to wake up to?

You once told me that you prayed all the time. So did I, Katie, but most of my prayers went unanswered; the obvious one being that you are not with me anymore. And without you, just who am I anyway? Nothing I have ever experienced compares with losing you. It is the worst thing a mother can go through: the loss of her precious child. I am on the cross, Katie. The finality of your death has put me there. Years from now, will people look up and still see me hanging there? What if I come down? Come down and then what? You will still not be here.

As I see it, there are several choices in front of me. I can be absent from my present life and the lives of others who need and love me and whom I need and love. I can give up the future and live in my past memories. Or I can accept the beauty and the bounty that I learned from being your mother and trust that I will survive without you. I do not know which choice will be mine, Katie.

I'm feeling very much that I want my own company. I do not feel up to talking with other people. I'm going to do what I feel I have to do to make it through my dark night. Recently I have heard horror stories about how people forget the memories that made up their life. What a terrible thought that was for me to hear. I took it to heart. So for right now, my only goal will be to get out of bed and write down some memories of my life so that I do not forget. I think I will begin when you were born, Katie; maybe throw in some of my childhood years while I'm at it. I need to do this. I need to survive. Put my thoughts on paper, my feet down on the floor and survive.

Love,
Mom

chapter *One*

Making the decision to have a child — it's momentous.
It is to decide forever to have your heart go
walking around outside your body.

~ELIZABETH STONE~
THE VILLAGE VOICE, 1985

Every mother can identify with that quote. Our children are our hearts. When Katie arrived $2\,1/2$ weeks before our first wedding anniversary, my husband, Dick, suggested we name her Catherine Marie. I was agreeable but only if we called her "Katie." My mother, however, thought it important to name children after some older family member, and since there were no Catherines on either side of the family, she asked me more than once, "Mary Jane, who is the baby being named after?" I always answered, "Saint Catherine."

As most mothers do with their new babies, I checked on Katie constantly. While she was sleeping I would place my ear close to her little pink chest and listen to her breathing in and out, in and out. Did that define me as neurotic? No, it defined me as a mother - gloriously happy one minute and six minutes away from being institutionalized the next - like the day Katie kicked off her umbilical cord and I saw a drop of blood. And wasn't that a sign right then that while we had once been attached, she also had her own and separate life to live? Good for Katie and good that this mom got it. All children need their own life and a good mother does not smother her own children. She does not make them her lifetime hobby because, believe me, children resent in the end when they are held too tightly; they know instinctively that too much "mommy knows best" undermines their confidence to sing their own song. A good mom will also not make her child accept a personal projection which does not fit his or her personality. Every mom might ask herself some questions that I learned to ask myself.

For example, maybe you wanted to be a stand up comedian and you make your child feel bad about being a serious student. Or maybe you are gifted athletically and have an extraverted temperament but not every one of your children is athletic or outgoing. Maybe one is and the others are all quiet and reserved and even klutzy. Or maybe you wanted to marry an investment banker and now you reject your daughter's choice of a sensitive poet who adores her.

I wanted Katie to apply to all the Ivy League Colleges. She did and was rejected. She did not care if she went to an Ivy; that was my projection, my unlived life, and she had to suffer because of it. When I finally understood what I had done I was shocked at myself and I apologized to Katie for it. It was unconscious on my part but she was the one who had to go through the process of applying and feeling rejected. We need to understand where our children are drawn, you and me, and delight in their individual talents as we guide them accordingly to make good choices for themselves.

Katie was always confident and knew what she wanted to do even at five years of age. That is an age when a child wants the attention of the opposite sex parent and will do anything to charm that parent to notice them. They are also getting interested in other

~Looking Back Reflections ~

I think it would have helped me to separate out my personal needs from what would have been more than "good enough" for our children. For sure it would have been less pressure had I realized that our children did not have to have the "best of everything." I let myself be too influenced by the culture. It did not do anyone much good.

people's bodies as well as their own. Katie was, developmentally, right on schedule and curious about her father's "anatomy."

On a summer vacation she decided to take an indirect route to investigate her interest while at the same time testing her dad's ability to handle a shock. We had just returned from the beach and wanted to shower away the sand. Behind the closed doors of the bedroom Dick and I chatted together nonchalantly as we yanked down our suits. In that split second, from behind a dresser "the hidden" Katie leapt out clapping wildly, laughing and shouting, SURPRISE! SURPRISE! SURPRISE!

Yes, Katie's mischievous side was arresting – it was part of her undeniable charm, and we saw it often as on this one particular Christmas. The children were pre-school age. It was 5:00 a.m. when I put on my robe and slippers and tiptoed down the hall to the children's rooms. Standing there motionless I could feel my adrenalin pumping. Finally, I just couldn't stand it any longer and I began clearing my throat louder and louder because in our house on Christmas there were more than just two kids in our home. Then the three of us ran laughing and hollering down the hall.

But we had a family rule. Everyone had to enter the living room at the same time. My husband, the king of teasers, had a routine that was simple: he tortured us all as much as he could for as long as he could before we entered the living room. First he pretended he was asleep. Second he crept out of bed and brushed his teeth in slow motion. After hearing enough, "DAD!" he said, "Okay, okay" and directly headed by himself to the living room. "Hey," he shouted, "Those cookies you left out for Santa were eaten!" Squeals of delight rang out as little feet went tearing down the hallway. They halted at the top of the stairs where Katie's brother Richard stood looking out into the living room.

Then came the yelling, "Look at all the stuff I got from Santa!" THIS WAS THE MOMENT. However, there was a small problem and of course Mrs. Claus saw it coming the night before when she suggested to Santa that all the presents needed to be wrapped. Santa Claus said "No, they never did that at the North Pole because Santa puts them under the tree, unwrapped, period!" Well, maybe dear old rational Santa wasn't as smart as Mrs. Claus after all because when Richard ran to Katie's "unwrapped" pile I mumbled, "Oh boy" just before I told young Richard that the toys in that pile were his sister's and not his.

With painful incredulity in his eyes, his face turned ruby and his cheeks puffed out. A second later he threw himself down on the floor next to his big sister Katie, who stood there wearing a big cherry lipped smile and the cowgirl hat that he thought was going to be his cowboy hat. And as much as I hated being an "I told you so" I knew my husband would be eating the mistletoe that Christmas, not just standing under it.

Katie had an innate perception. When she was almost six and Richard was four, we were in the grocery store when he leaped out of the shopping cart and licked some yellow liquid off the floor. Horrified, I scooped him up and ran screaming to the water fountain. When everyone settled down - mostly me - Katie asked if I felt mad at Richard, or was I just scared that he was hurt? Stunned by her sagacious perception, I simply said, "Both, Sweetheart." She responded, and demurely I might add, "Oh I see, Mommy." Thinking back now I realize how much of my temper has been about fear: fear of losing what I loved most; fear that I couldn't control something bad from happening; fear that someone I loved dearly would suddenly die.

Freud was right on with his understanding that anxiety is the ego's response to the threat of a potential loss of a love object. For my part, the fear was unconscious and it presented as anger whenever the kids impetuously rode their bikes in the street, ran with sticks or threw things at one another. If they got sick I was terrified. "Oh, you're sick!" I would shout in a frightened, out of control voice. When I was premenstrual, my pitch was elevated, because what lies in the unconscious is exacerbated (not made up) during that time. Let's face it, hormones are powerful and hormone replacement therapy isn't a billion dollar industry for nothing.

The meat of our story will now begin at Katie's graduation ceremony from the eighth grade at St. Monica's. This turning point of thirteen and fourteen is an important stage in our personality development.

So on that graduation night, as I watched Katie addressing this assembly of teachers, parents and classmates, I reflected on the strength of her sense of self, the strength of both her feeling and thinking function, and the strength of her honesty. She took the majority of awards that night, the math medal being her most satisfying achievement. Dick and I

~Looking Back Reflections ~

I believe it would have helped my stress levels had I shared my anxieties with the other mothers who were my friends. Maybe my honesty would have helped them to share their stresses. I was also blind to hormonal interplay which made me more reactive emotionally, especially when I was tired. Taking a nap now and then and ordering a pizza instead of thinking that I had to make every dinner from scratch didn't help either.

were thrilled for her. But during the ceremony I also felt myself drifting back to the memory of what my own life had been like at the age of thirteen. It was a story very different than Katie's that I now share in this letter to her.

July 15, 1999
Dear Katie,

The poet, Muriel Rukeyser, wrote a poem about a sculptor named Kathe Kollwitz. She inquired in the poem, rhetorically, "What would happen if one woman told the truth about her life?" To which she responded, "The world would split open." So, dear Katie, since I was reflecting on your graduation being far different than my graduation, let me share exactly how dissimilar it was.

I won the award for leadership that night but the evening was eclipsed by what had occurred the previous year, when I was in the 7th grade. It was May 2, 1960, and an important spring day for our little school because the new archbishop of the diocese was visiting. Everyone looked especially neat that morning: the boys' blue plaid ties were spotless, navy blue pants creased. The girls' maroon uniforms were immaculate, white blouses starched, and if you were on the Safety Patrol Team, badges were shined and we were required to wear them, making me even happier because your mother was the Captain. As excitement levels increased, with pushing, shoving and laughing, my teacher quietly approached me. "Mary Jane," she told me, "Sister Marceline wants to see you." Being wildly optimistic by nature, I thought our principal had chosen me to assist with the day's festivities. But that thought vanished when I reached her doorway and saw, standing next to her mammoth oak desk, my wide-eyed eleven year old brother Frank and three feet from him, my mother. Oh, God, something awful must have happened because first, Mom never came to school and second, she would never refuse to look directly at Frank or me and only stare blankly out the window. Yes, Katie, even in profile I knew Mom's light was gone.

My eyes darted from Sister Marceline's face to my mother's face. I tried to read them for emotional clues. My mind raced with questions about what had happened. I figured that whatever happened, it was very serious. Maybe it was even unspeakable. I felt frightened. Then my mother silently gestured with her hand and pointed at the door. Her face, drawn and tired, told me it was time to leave. I turned and looked at Sister Marceline, who always reminded me of bamboo: tall, thin and perpetually leaning over. While most of the kids were afraid of her, I wasn't because I knew Sister liked me. Today a hint of kindness was present in her normally stern face. She looked at me and then in a voice barely above a whisper, she said to my mother, "I'll check in with you later, Mrs. Hurley."

Outside, an idling blue sedan waited for us. Somberly the three of us slid into the back seat. Your Aunt Eileen, then just seven years old, was seated next to the female driver and humming MIC-KEY-MOUSE. This unidentified woman drove us home, where on the front porch stood our favorite uncle of all time, Uncle Charlie. But on this day he wasn't smiling and joking around like he normally did. "Come for a ride with me, Mary Jane and Francis," was all that he said so like the good kids we were, my brother and I got into his car. That's when my brother leaned toward me and with cupped hands to my ear, breath hot and steamy, he whispered, "Do you think Grandpop died, Mary Jane?" An obvious question given that Grandpop was old and lived with us.

Before I could respond, Uncle Charlie pulled over to the side of the road we called "The Back Road" because it wasn't paved. He slowly turned around and stared at us for heaven knows how long. I stared back sensing something horrible was happening. "Mary Jane and Francis, I'm sorry to have to tell you something very sad ... your father had a bad accident today." We sat as still as figurines while our normally never serious uncle inhaled an audibly deep breath.

"Children, your father died this morning." That was when Uncle Charlie started making choking sounds, shaking, crying and blowing his nose all at the same time. I locked onto his red sad face like radar on an F-14 as the agony in his eyes shot straight to my heart. That's when my brother joined in and sobbed so mournfully that all I can remember was rubbing his back and repeating, "It's okay Francis, it's okay." You see, Katie, that's what we called your Uncle Frank when we were young, Francis. Just then the ignition turned over and the gears shifted - Uncle Charlie had spun the car around toward Homestead Avenue to the house which after this day would cease being a home for me.

When the car stopped, Frank leaped out and took the front porch steps two at a time before disappearing inside. Because I felt suspicious of Uncle Charlie's story, I walked to the rear of the house sniffing around like an FBI agent for proof of an accident. There in our driveway sat my dad's truck. I ran my hand over the bumper, the hood, and the two large van doors in the back. Where was the damage? I didn't see any dents or signs of an accident. Feeling confused, I turned to see two girls from my 7th grade class headed in my direction. Still in their school uniforms, they carried the little American flags for the Archbishop's welcoming parade, the parade I never got to see. "What happened to my father? I asked then. "Do you know what kind of accident he had?" The more outgoing girl responded,

"Oh, Mary Jane, I don't know if we should tell you." Well, she didn't tell me, and I felt immediately angry, Katie, because here were two girls who knew something about someone I loved and I didn't have a damn clue. Just then some of my cousins came running down the driveway. "I have to go; my cousins are here," was all I said. Kids are kids; my cousins and I started playing tag. Just minutes into the game my mother called me to the back door. "Yes, Mom?" She hit me hard across the face, "Can't you even grieve one day for your father?" I just stood there, Katie, stunned and horrified. She had never struck me before.

Of course now I realize mom was in shock, and I feel bad about that, nevertheless that's no excuse for what she did to me on this tragic day. The psychoanalyst Alice Miller, famous for writing about parents' aggression toward children has this to say, "The greatest cruelty that can be inflicted on children is to refuse to let them express their anger and suffering except at the risk of losing their parents' love and affection." [1] I, like many children, stuffed down my angry feelings and instead walked into the living room, removed my parakeet "Nippy" from his cage and placed him on my shoulder for consolation. While rubbing my cheek against his soft yellow feathers, I started crying and that's when the little sociopath bit me. Yes, Katie, while his name was Nippy, he usually nipped others, not me. I immediately stopped crying and vowed then to my thirteen year old self that I would never cry again over my father, my mother or my stupid bird as long as I lived. I put him back into his cage and went to answer the ringing front door bell.

Standing there was a crowd; some people I knew, some I didn't. Like ants carrying crumbs, in single file they marched inside, arms laden with all kinds of food, especially sweets. On pretty lace doilies the tasty treats sat in the kitchen: chocolate cakes, cream puffs and homemade butter cookies. But while they were tempting and delicious looking, I didn't take a one. I thought that shoving goodies into my mouth at a time like this

---

1 *For Your Own Good*, p. 106

would be a sign of pure weakness, an infantile pacifier for grief. I went back into the living room, where squatting down in front of my sister Eileen was Mom. Eileen's First Holy Communion was planned for the coming weekend and my little sister was talking sweetly to Mom about it. Frank was there too. "Eileen," Mom said, "your father isn't here anymore."

"Where did he go?" my sister innocently asked, her pretty little lips pouting. "He went to the angels," Mom responded. My poor little sister, who was fearful about most things to begin with, jumped up and ran to her room. I followed on her heels. "What are you doing, Eileen?" I asked gently as I watched her ferreting under her bed. In a voice barely audible she responded,

"I'm looking for Daddy, Mary Jane."

For many days we were kept home from school. How long? I don't know; I've repressed so much but I do recall staring out the window, playing with my jacks and listening to 45 rpm records, especially "Sixteen Candles," the first record I ever owned, sung by the Crests and bought by my dad. Listening to it I started thinking of all the great things he had given me, small in the world's eyes, big to a thirteen year old: a six button Benny coat with a beaver collar he carried in after work one day.

Then there was a bottle of perfume he said a movie star friend of his had given to him just for me. A red rug he had woven himself with my initials "MJH" right in the middle was a prized possession. I sat there remembering everything about him, how he taught me to dance, play cards and tell jokes. Yes, I remembered, but I wasn't feeling. I was in shock. I remember the nuns coming and going. I remember we weren't allowed to watch TV, see any newspapers, or have any friend over and we didn't know why. That was, until the day my mother allowed me to visit a girlfriend in the neighborhood.

We usually hung out in her bedroom. When her mother called this friend downstairs to set the dinner table, I stopped at her bureau to comb my hair. There, tucked into the dresser mirror, was a newspaper clipping whose title said it all, "Man Leaps from Bridge to his Death." And that's the way I found out how my poor father had died.

Shock and then anger cut through me. "Why would she display that on her mirror? What kind of friend would do such a thing? Obviously she knew about my father, why hadn't she told me?" With no explanation to anyone, I left. My next memory was as at my dad's funeral Mass nine long days later. The delay

was because of a debate among the head clergy about
whether a suicide - my father - was worthy of being buried in blest ground. That was a Catholic Church rule back
then. My God, my poor mother, who was so religious,
must have been in double agony. To add to her pain, an
anonymous woman called on the day of the funeral and
said to my mother, who answered the phone, "Did you
see him after he jumped?" Can you imagine, Katie? My
mother never did see him; the head nurse at Our Lady
of Lourdes Hospital, a good hearted nun, urged Mom
not to, "Remember him as he was, Mrs. Hurley." Years
later Mom told me she had always regretted that decision. I don't know what I would have done under those
circumstances.

In church, listening to the seventh and eighth
grade girls singing sweetly away in the choir room felt
surreal to me, like I was looking at a movie, because I
wasn't with them. That's what it feels like in this stage
of bereavement, like you are watching someone else's
life. But, Katie, this wasn't someone else's life, instead it
was my life and I was in a pew in the main body of the
church at my dad's funeral. Like Seraphim, the girls
sang the beautiful requiem Mass: *Panis angelicus* and *Pie
Jesu Domine, dona eis requiem, O sweet Lord Jesus, grant them*

rest. I thought how only a week before, a boy in my class named Peter had lost his father and now there would be two of us at St. John's School who had no dad. I knew that made us different. I knew that made me different.

The priest ended the service with a blessing of peace. Peace? Who could think of peace today? Clearly not my mother because when Grandpop began weeping - something I'd never seen him do before - my mother's words rang out, "Cut it out, Pop!" I felt stung and embarrassed for poor Grandpop. Didn't he have every right to show his sorrow? He loved our father as everyone did. Something had changed and become dark in my mother; it made me leery to be near her after that. But now that I'm older I understand that these circumstances must have been a horror for her. That day I thought she was simply angry at Grandpop. Now I think her anger was about my father and she was terrified for her life and ours. The Church's questioning Daddy's right for a proper burial must have been excruciating because from that day forth my mother attended Mass every single morning, undoubtedly worried about his soul. She also became rail thin, smiled less and was more quiet than usual.

When you and Rich were both under ten, I told

you some of this. I dreaded doing it, you know, but I dreaded more your hearing about it from someone else simply because I wanted to be a person in your life whom both of you could count on to give information to you straight, about anything. A lie, even a white one, would throw a shadow of doubt on every previous story and every one to come. Besides, I think children deserve to hear the truth in a language they can understand no matter how uncomfortable a parent is relaying it. Frank says Mom told him about the suicide; I can't speak to that but Eileen found out six years later when she, Mom and I were washing the dishes and the subject of suicide came up. That's when Eileen said, offhandedly, "Oh, people go straight to hell when they do that." Seconds later the sound of a slap rang out over the sink, stopping the exchange. I remember you winced hearing that part of the story, Katie, just as I did witnessing it, because that kind of behavior was foreign to you - neither your father nor I ever raised a hand to you or Rich. Your dad knew also, and first hand, how damaging that was to a child's sense of self worth.

After Mom turned her back, I whispered to your Aunt Eileen, my then thirteen-year-old sibling, "Don't ever say that again, Eileen, that's how Daddy died." Yes,

Katie, that was the moment my sister found out, the moment I realized she knew nothing about our father's death and the moment I realized how I hated family secrets and pain inflicted in the name of parental authority. So now on top of the first vow to myself never to cry over my mother, my father or my bird, I made a second vow never to take orders from anyone concerning my own life.

No one was ever the same after Daddy died and who ever is really and how could we be? Even our dog became a different dog. She sat in the driveway howling and making a terrible sound for weeks. She bugged me with her yapping, crying and eating all the time. Seeing that mutt so miserable made me very angry because it reminded me how much I wanted things to go back to the way they used to be when my father was alive. I would look at that animal and think how I used to love her; my dad brought her home as a puppy in a rain storm zipped up in his jacket. But now I displaced my anger onto that dumb little beast; my adaptation because kids don't want to be angry with someone they love. I was angry at my dad; crushed and confused by what he did, but how can a kid be angry at someone who isn't even there anymore? How can a kid be angry with someone they love so much? And how can a kid understand personal feelings surrounding such a complex and traumatizing situation? In two words: they cannot; their age prohibits that level of sophisticated thinking and processing.

When I was in my forties, Mom told me that I was the one of her children who was most like Dad. By then I worked as a psychotherapist, Katie, choosing the counseling field to help other people learn to talk about their feelings. I thought maybe if someone had helped our father talk about his feelings he would still be with us. I guess I could say Frank Vincent Hurley Senior gave me my profession. So Mom saying I was the most like him felt amazing because I knew how much she loved him. Intuitively I always knew my father and I were alike but it felt comforting knowing Mom realized it, too. You remember how you thought I was funny, Katie? Well, so did he and was himself very comedic. Once, at a family party when I was three years old, he picked me up, put me on the kitchen table and asked me to sing, 'Don't roll those bloodshot eyes at me.' My aunts and uncles were hysterical laughing.

So, dear Heart, I guess it's true what poet and writer Anne Sexton once said, "It doesn't matter who my father was; it matters who I remember he was." I remember my dad, Katie, as the hero of my child's heart. To this day the smell of olive oil warming in a sauce pan makes me think of his Sunday cooking. I felt cherished by my father as your dad cherished you and Rich but, Katie, when he died, I had to deny my grief because if I had not, I would have had to acknowledge what really occurred: that he was gone forever. The unspoken stigma attached to suicide in the 1960's didn't help, and not too much was understood then about psychology, psychiatry and depression, so forget about consoling words or hugs from anyone, it just didn't happen. Believe me, Sweetheart; death by one's own hand produces a heavy silence of enormous weight that just hangs over everything.

Years later, Mom spoke more about him, saying the Pacific Islands had been cruel to the U. S. Marines. She told us our father fought in Guadalcanal, Iwo Jima, and Okinawa. He was held prisoner on one of them and made to watch the death of his entire platoon - one-by-one - because he was their Sergeant in Command and the enemy thought he knew something. Poor Daddy, he didn't know anything. I think it's a fair assessment to say that the psychic disturbance his mind and spirit suffered during those long years in the war just never left him - an undiagnosed Post-Traumatic Stress Disorder.

Unquestionably the trauma of his leaving
remained with our family. Mom said dark memories
from being in World War II ate daddy alive from the
inside. Well, his absence ate me alive from the inside
too, Katie. It makes me wonder just how many other
men and women died by their own hand because the
trauma never died inside.

After our father's death Mom rarely mentioned
his name except to sigh and say "my Frank." Mom never
cried openly. Occasionally she mentioned that Francis
cried every night. "Your brother's pillow was wet with
his tears again this morning." Then she would shake her
head. I never asked Mom exactly what she meant, but I
figured there was only room in our house for one person crying and my brother got first dibs. So, like Mom,
I didn't cry either. Too bad I didn't check it out with her
about tears - hers, everyone's and mine because what
someone says might not be heard the same way the person saying it wants it to be. Meaning that she might have
thought it was okay for me to cry. It would have helped
me not carry it silently for so long.

After Dad's death, no day seemed the right one to
talk about him, except Christmas Day, which made that
holiday awful. You just can't save up that amount of sor-

row and squeeze it into one twenty-four hour period. I think many families suffer terribly after a big loss, Katie. Maybe the pain is because a sibling has cut off all connections with the entire family or, God help us, someone was murdered or sent to jail. Everyone feels their personal pain in their own specific way. From high school days and into graduate school my dreams were flooded with recurring dreams of being a hero, always trying to save someone with my brave dog, Rin-Tin-Tin, a popular show from the 1950's about a boy and his German Shepherd dog that my unconscious mind adopted. This amazing dog and I would stand on a bridge. I gave him his command, "Yoohhh Rinty." Then the mighty Shepherd would dive into the dark water with me right behind him swimming down, down into the depths.

I approached Mom once and said I wished she had talked more about our father. "I wanted you children to have a normal life," was her response. I sighed when I heard that because deep down I knew that was true. Sometimes it's a no-win for parents: they do what they think is best in the moment and years later the children are upset. Oh, God, it must have been so difficult for your grandmother, Katie. Raising three kids with no job, no husband and no dreams was a slam against every

Post-World War II hope a person could have. One day I told your grandmother I needed to discuss something serious with her. "Mom," I said, "you should never have hit us kids when we were young and I think you need to apologize for doing it." She glared at me, long, hard and silent.

Since that day I have spoken to many clients who said that their parents hit them to control their behavior. Belts, switches, hangers, spoons, an open hand. It always horrifies me. These grown children today have, more often than not, stored up that anger toward the parent and taken it out unconsciously on other people, usually the spouse. Sometimes the "taking it out" is in the subtle form of not trusting people, even their mate, or in explosive rages with name calling and insults shouted. The generation that raised the baby-boomers really believed it was okay to hit their children and society concurred. It was not okay. It is always wrong when parents loose control of their hands or their mouths.

So dear Katie, the bottom line is that we parents are not perfect. Your grandmom wasn't and I wasn't. She never expected to be made a widow at forty-three years of age and raise the three of us alone. My mother was faithfully present in our lives. She cooked, cleaned and listened whenever we needed to talk about anything. She had a quiet strength and never looked for any glory. She and we must wrestle with our human nature and our darker selves. We struggle and we struggle and we learn to forgive. Seven times seventy we learn to forgive.

My parents, like most parents, did the best they could given their own demons, histories and abilities. I hope that I as a parent did a good job, Katie. But I know that I made many mistakes, too. So where I disappointed or hurt you I now ask, please forgive me, Sweetheart. It was never, ever my intention.

Love,
Mom

~Looking Back Reflections ~

Thinking about those days now I realize that I was always worried about my mother. As a result I did not process my own grief about my father. I was a parentified child who tried to take her father's place in the family - as unbelievable as that may sound. But it was never my job to replace my absent father as a parent. Trying to do so caused me to sever parts of my child self that needed a forum and a place to develop, grieve and just be a kid.

Before we knew it, the time for taking high school entrance exams had begun. Katie sat for those offered at the local Catholic high school and one private Catholic school for girls, The Academy of Notre Dame de Namur in Villanova, Pennsylvania. Unexpectedly, she won a full four-year academic scholarship to that academy. She sobbed reading the acceptance letter knowing an 'all girl's school' meant 'a no boys school.' When the day arrived to tour the Academy and make the decision as to whether Katie would be going there or not, the principle, Sister Regina Finnegan, said that in all of the years this academy administered the exam, no girl had ever scored higher than Katie. Well, even though Katie was not completely okay with the "all girl's" thing, she realized that her parents were not going to refuse such a generous gift.

And while Katie's intelligence won her the scholarship, it was her emotional and psychological ability that drew others to her. Her ego, composed of conscious perceptions and feelings, was also progressing beautifully and she chose her spots strategically, rationally, and calmly to use or surrender that ego. This judiciousness would undoubtedly help Katie manage her life because when the ego develops properly and is itself highly individuated, one becomes a better adjusted person capable of dealing competently with the hard times.

During Katie's four years at Notre Dame, her spirit and

integrity blossomed in the friendships, the academics and the leadership positions she held. Positions such as captain of the basketball team and officer in the student council. Students and faculty alike admired Katie, quickly recognizing her kindness, directness and compassion. The nuns loved her madly and still talk about how exceptional and funny Katie was. They especially liked talking about the time she drove too fast in the rain and caused an accident.

July 20, 1999
Dear Katie,

I remember Sister Regina telling me how you called the convent, yelling hysterically into the phone, "OH GOD, SISTER REGINA, I HIT A MAN WITH MY CAR!" Sister Regina, bless her, jumped into the school's van shouting to the other nuns huddling in the convent door, "PRAY FOR KATIE BRANT, SHE JUST RAN OVER A MAN!" Well, it turned out you had hit a man but he was driving his car. But you had them all going there for sure.

My precious Katie, did you know I sometimes drive over to that beautiful old mansion at Notre Dame, roll down the car window and watch the girls on the playing

fields? Their blue plaid uniforms, their happy, youth-
ful faces erase all the years for me. Sometimes I actually
think I see you when some spirited, pony-tailed straw-
berry blond holds her lacrosse stick high in the air and
runs like the wind. Sometimes I just close my eyes and it
feels like yesterday, long ago and far away. And sometimes, I just sit there and weep.

Yes, Katie, I would return to those days in a heartbeat. Yes, Dear Heart, I wish we could do it all again.

Love,
Mom

chapter *Two*

I am circling around God, around the ancient tower,
and I have been circling for a thousand years
and I still don't know if I am a falcon,
or a great storm, or a great song.

~RAINER MARIA RILKE~

Being a mother changed my life from being about me to being about my children. Maybe I am a falcon, for sure there is a hurricane inside, and I often feel a song in my heart. But when the fall of 1988 arrived and Katie left for Colgate University in upstate New York to begin her college experience, I felt my life cave in. No one prepares us mothers for the day the child we have taken care of and loved for so many years leaves us. That's the way it goes and when it happens, and it is supposed to happen, it is devastating.

One day Katie called from college, "Mom, I'm having fun and even doing volunteering in the community!" I asked her was she eating all right, sleeping all right?

"Well I am but sometimes I have this weird feeling that makes me a little dizzy, but then it passes. The nurses at the infirmary said it's related to stress or hormones." Never wanting to undermine Katie's confidence - especially now that she was a college girl - I told her to stay on top of it and return to the infirmary if it reoccurs. Her father thought she had found the college beer keg.

That same fall my sister Eileen's five-year-old daughter, Jennifer, needed an open-heart operation for a serious condition she had had since her birth. Jenny had already undergone several other heart surgeries, all of them scary, but this one was the most serious with a twenty percent chance she would not make it. Jennifer was never a well child. She suffered an impaired heart from birth and her first surgery was performed when she was just one day old. Mom lived with my sister's family while Jenny recuperated and was heroic in her efforts to comfort the baby, Bruce and Eileen. Only a few years before Mom had taken care of Eileen who was recuperating from the removal of a cancerous neck tumor. Mom was wonderful in any crisis.

So after the necessary blood matches were made and masses were offered, the surgery commenced. But sadly and tragically, on November 4, 1988, precious Jennifer died during the operation. My sister called from the hospital to tell me. "Mary, Jenny didn't make it. You have to go tell Mom." So my husband Dick, my brother Frank and I drove to New Jersey to Mom's house. I watched the trees pass by; I watched the back of my bother's and my husband's heads turning towards one another while they talked about Eileen and her husband Bruce. I let my thoughts be about Jennifer. I thought about how adorable she was, delicate and sweet in every way. I thought about how she would sing little nursery songs and eat clams on the half shell. I thought about how in less than six years she had brought back my mother's smile and playfulness, accomplishing what I could not do since I was a teenager: make Mom look and feel happier. I also felt uncertain that we should be the people telling my mother about Jenny.

When we pulled up to my childhood front porch, Frank, Dick and I walked up the front steps like mountain climbers roped together for survival. I rang the bell. Mom peeked through the blinds; she knew why we were there; she snapped them shut; refused us entrance. "Mom, please open the door." Frank, Dick and I looked at one another. Minutes later we heard the latch move. Through the small opening in the doorway Mother's pale blue eyes peered out as she simultaneously backed away, whispering, then shouting, "NO, NO, DON'T SAY IT!" I pushed the door open, reached for her hand,

"Mom, she didn't make it, Jenny didn't make it." Mom began to cry and her legs gave out from under her. We grabbed her then, held her up and close until I thought her spirit would completely expire.

The magnitude of this loss was devastating for my mother. She loved that little girl like her very own child and that wasn't just speculation on my part, Mom told me that herself right before Jennifer's surgery. I did not know what to do or what to say. I searched like a mad woman for answers, and thinking of the doctor, who never said he was sorry, I shook my fist in the air. Then I shook my fist in the air at God. As we drove home that night I thought to myself, where was life's fairness? "Live a good life and God will reward you?" Eileen and Bruce no longer had their little girl and this poor grandmother, this formidable woman of faith already had had enough suffering for ten lifetimes and now Jenny, her precious grandchild, was dead. Mom couldn't stop crying. This was a terrible first for me because I had never seen my mother weep before and it prompted a rush of tenderness and overwhelming sadness within me. I also felt more vulnerable to bad things happening.

Now Jenny was gone; I was heartbroken, depressed and disappointed in God. Linda Carter, who was my sister's best friend from childhood, was there to help me comfort Eileen throughout the funeral day. In a little over an hour, Jenny's Mass of the Resurrection was complete. Now came the dreaded drive to the cemetery. At the grave site a large group of family and friends stood close together, a solid structure, the Great Wall of China, they huddled close simply to hold back a flood of sorrow. The funeral director handed each mourner a balloon: orange and blue, green and violet, pink and white for five-year old Jennifer was a rainbow of color.

The air went silent; the faces somber and bereft. The priest sprinkled the holy water upon this precious angel's casket, said a final prayer for her tender innocent soul. When he nodded his head, we had our signal to release all the balloons at once. Higher and higher they flew toward heaven. Smaller and smaller the balloons quickly disappeared from sight. Our little Jenny was with God. Please dear Lord, strengthen her parents and my mother for the days to come. It was the only thing that I could pray.

~Looking Back Reflections ~

I see now that the death of Jennifer was another huge loss for me but again I bottled it up inside of me. Being the first born in my family also made me assume that it was my job to take care of everyone else. When my grief surfaced, I pushed it aside because that was what I had learned to do after the loss of my father. Now I know better. Now I know that there are the known stages many people feel after a death, or whatever is felt as a loss for us.

Initially we experience denial or shock. It can last for weeks. Next anger erupts. This emotion rarely knows where to land. More often than not the anger is to cover our despair, anxiety, pain and grief. Next we often begin bargaining with God that we will do anything to live or not have to carry this disease or suffer this experience or loss. Next a depression can follow and with it a profound yearning and searching for the deceased or the lost situation and the life that we once had. This stage can last for months and even years. (Elizabeth Kubler-Ross, M.D. and John Bolby, Ph.D.)

Naturally these stages have much to do with what or whom we have lost and the degree of our personal attachment to the individual or the situation. When the loss is a death we may begin to understand, at least intellectually, that we are mortal beings and that loss will be experienced by all of us as we journey though our lives. Logically we understand death is part of life but emotionally we somehow think that we can escape it.

The loss of Jennifer was monumental for everyone. I felt woefully inadequate in comforting Eileen or my mother because no one, not even a big sister or daughter, can give much to a mother who has lost her precious child. That mother or grandmother wants only one thing: that child back in her arms. The years 1988 and 1989 were sad and dark periods of mourning for our family and they changed me a great deal. My friend Lennie and my analyst Alex helped me as much as I would let them. I refer to these days now as my seasons of discontent because I had to rethink every principle and value I held dear. I learned that my idealism didn't work anymore. I learned that control is a miserable illusion I believe was invented by the devil himself. I learned I had no choice other than insanity if I didn't accept situations and people I could not change. I learned I had to accept the challenges that my fate delivered which brought me to my knees and, yes, I had to accept the comfort that tears offered and allow myself, for once, to weep.

By Memorial Day weekend of 1989, six months after Jenny's death, our daughter Katie had completed her first year of college and our family boarded a flight for a trip to Europe. After a visit to LeSacre Coeur in Montmartre, Paris, we stopped for lunch at an outside cafe. Before finishing, Katie became quiet for a moment, and then looked blankly away. "What was that, Mom?" she said, rejoining the conversation. It was subtle, this little disconnect.

"Are you doing okay, Honey?" I asked.

"Just that same funny feeling I sometimes got at school, Mom." Then Katie looked away again and while I had never seen a petite mal seizure before in my life, it crossed my mind that maybe that was what just happened. But I shrugged it off as mother vigilance.

After lunch Rich and Katie took the metro back to the hotel. During the ride, a thief stole Katie's wallet and the fifty bucks in it. She was visibly perturbed, Rich told us. He added, "When Katie started talking on the train, her thoughts were all mixed up!" I was concerned. Days later we were back home when Katie and her friend Kristen went grocery shopping for me. In the checkout line, Katie became agitated and confused, "Where did we get all of this stuff?" she kept repeating, "Where did we get all of these groceries?"

Being so worked up was completely out of character for Katie. Alarmed, we called her internist who administered an EEG the following day, calling soon afterwards with the results. The EEG was prompted on my mentioning the way she looked away at lunch and her confusion. The results came back: temporal lobe activity; it indicates seizures. Bottom line: Katie may have epilepsy. Katie cried for an hour thinking her driver's license would be revoked. An MRI was scheduled for Thursday, "just to make sure there is nothing else in there."

At 10:30 p.m. two days later - it was a Thursday - her doctor phoned with the results. I answered, but Katie pleaded, "Mom, please give me the phone!" I handed it over.

"Katie, we see something on the MRI"; the doctor said. "It could be a tumor." No one spoke but the silence was deafening. Finally, Dick broke into the quiet,

"We'll figure out what to do; we'll deal with it." Katie left the room and immediately called her friends - a healthy response to that horrific announcement. The following morning, Friday, began our accelerated immersion into the difficult maze of medical specialists. Dick called a physician we knew to ask about Katie's chances. His response was negative. "The statistics are bad for this." When Dick told me what he said, I shouted, "Never talk to him again!" Believe me no one wants to hear such a negative response in a newly diagnosed situation. Anger is also a typical reaction to fear. What to do; who to call? No one understands the medical maze of a first diagnosis. We were lucky when unexpectedly a doctor friend heard of our plight and told us to call Children's Hospital of Philadelphia. Katie's internist concurred. Telling us explicitly what to do gave us some direction and some language with which to do so.

We pushed ahead and met with the neurosurgeon at Children's Hospital of Philadelphia that Friday. He seemed confident. "I have a great deal of experience with this kind of right temporal lobe surgery; if one has a brain tumor, it's the best placement for an operation." We asked, "Why did the tumor present now?" He told us that Katie had "a sleeping tumor" discovered only when it was large enough to press down on areas of the brain that indicated its presence. Then I asked the question I posed to every doctor I met for the next ten years, a question that tortured me and that my daughter eventually pleaded with me to stop asking,

"How did Katie get a brain tumor? Did a fall years ago cause a head trauma? Was it the environment? Did she have abnormal cells?"

"We just don't know" was his response. The surgery was scheduled for the following Monday morning.

Back home Dick made additional phone calls while I sat on Katie's floor and opened my old psychology text. I stared at pictures and diagrams: brain stem, cerebellum, right temporal lobe, frontal lobe. When I looked up, Dick was there and crying. Crying? Why was he crying, was he giving up? He seemed without hope and it made me angry.

Katie's surgery day commenced on the following Monday, June 16, 1989. She pleaded with the nurses to shave only a conservative amount of hair away. After she kissed us good bye she marched to the gurney with her shoulders back, her courage intact, and her undaunted spirit prevailing. Then, we waited.

The time a family paces, prays and perseveres during a child's surgery or a loved one's operation is frightening. For our family the fear walked through the door, wore a scary face and pulled up a chair.

Seven hours later, in post surgical recovery,

Katie opened her eyes, smiled, and asked for a cold Diet Coke. I yanked one from my purse. The following afternoon much of Katie's gorgeous red hair, streaked with bright shades of blond, now lay in large clumps stuck to the bandages - so much for earnest requests. As I stood over her in ICU, I kissed her precious forehead while pretending to move the hair away from her eyes. What I was really doing was picking the hair out of the gauze and stuffing it into my jeans pocket. Concurrently a six-page loveletter from Katie's new boyfriend arrived by fax and with it, two-dozen long stem roses: twelve red; twelve white. She asked me to read her fax. "Why not wait until you can read it in private, Sweetheart?"

She didn't want to, "Mom, please, I need you to do it right now!"

~Looking Back Reflections ~

I think this was one of the things that I did right: appreciate the appearance of someone special showing up just when our family needed extra help. Gratitude for "the angels" who appeared out of nowhere. Because of the way I was raised I thought it would have been an imposition to actually ask somebody for help. Now I know better. Now I think asking for help would have ameliorated some pain.

The fax was full of young love. I held in my tears of joy for now Katie had a special fellow to hold in her thoughts instead of a preoccupation with cancer. I felt the timing was miraculous.

We all appreciate the challenge of raising children under "normal" conditions but no one even mentions anything else after a life threatening diagnosis like cancer, divorce, or a son or daughter being shipped off to war is on the table. The relativity scale for any complaints is obvious: they don't get floor time. But we all know that regular life goes on even when a serious situation descends upon a family.

If your child is on drugs, or terminally ill, or dad has run off to be with another woman, or mom has breast cancer, things like clean your room, mow the lawn, be home by midnight, no eggs in the refrigerator, or mom is tired just don't get on the docket. In our case, Richard was a senior in high school and gearing up to visit colleges. That reality demanded that Dick and I also focus on the best match in schools for him and the accompanying stress that the college application process challenges a student and their families with also.

Richard loved his sister and, like the rest of us, was scared for her and all of us. The crisis on our family table was demanding and while "regular life" was over as we knew it with Katie's brain tumor diagnosis, we were no different than other families confronting loss or potential loss, we had to deal with regular day-to-day living which waits for no man, woman or child.

Five days after Katie's initial operation, she, Dick, and I met with a radiologist and oncologist to discuss Katie's post-surgical protocol - the plan for combating her disease. The regime was daunting: she would undergo radiation for forty-five consecutive days and chemotherapy for thirteen and one-half months. The barrage of dreadful side effects was endless; particularly that the radiation could cause a secondary cancer, deafness or stroke, and chemotherapy could cause sterility.

Unsure about how to proceed, Dick again consulted with Katie's oncologist at Children's Hospital of Philadelphia who suggested we 'consider' a second opinion while discretely handing Dick a list of names of local physicians. Dick expected the doctors to be other radiologists and oncologists. When he called them, he discovered the doctors on the list were all surgeons. Surgeons? Why surgeons? Something didn't add up here. Back to the oncologist he went.

After a short discussion ensued, this ethical physician suggested Dick have a discussion with Katie's surgeon and ask a few additional questions. He didn't elaborate further, just raised his eyebrows in a suspicious manner. Back to the surgeon Dick went.

It no time Dick connected the dots: something was wrong. "Doctor," he asked, "how much of the tumor did you actually remove from Katie?" With great pomposity the surgeon responded,

"I removed a tumor the size of an egg!"

"An egg? But Katie's tumor was the size of a fist. What about the remaining tumor you left?"

"NO ONE ELSE COULD DO BETTER!" the surgeon shouted.

"You arrogant bastard," Dick hissed, "You lied to us. You didn't get the whole tumor out!"

More confusion set in. Start the radiation and chemotherapy? Go for more surgery? Dick's and my stress mounted and our fears escalated. People often hide the darker side of monumental stressors, about the panic that sets into a family confronting this type of horror. But if I talk about what happened to us it may alert and help someone else know that mine fields abound during these types of frightening circumstances. Our family is no different than yours.

Carl Jung once said that the gods from Olympus visit us during crises; well they visited me, all right, with the god of war leading the group. Primal fear enveloped me; I plummeted into an emotionally regressed state. That is not an unusual response to a possible death sentence or an actual death. Unconsciously I felt as I did at thirteen years of age because this frightening situation mirrored the terror I experienced after my father died. It was as if I picked up from that date with every year in between gone because the unconscious part of me remembered that one day my father suddenly disappeared - the man I loved beyond measure - so who could say that my dear firstborn child, whom I loved beyond my own life, would not also leave me? Was that a stretch? No way, that was what could happen and that was what did happen.

An internal whirling dervish possessed me. I could not sleep and I had little desire for food. In ten days I weighed 114 pounds, the exact weight I had been as a seventh grader when my father died. Yes, I had entered a depression and I did not even know it because it did not appear as a depression: my affect was an agitated one. Instead of my being down and incapacitated, the way many depressions present; I went out of myself and some days, felt out of my mind with anxiety and worry.

July 30, 1999
Dear Katie,

What a hard summer it was when you were diagnosed. I struggled with a smile on my face as I dropped from a size 6 to a size 2. On one visit to see my mother, she said that I looked just as she did when my father died. Even that made me mad because my skin was also as thin as parchment.

Remember that awful surgeon? Did I ever tell you the relief I felt when your father challenged his hubris? After that confrontation your dad returned to the referring oncologist, thanked him for his "suggestions" and asked for names of the "best" pediatric neurosurgeons in the US. Yes, we were all deeper into the medical maze by then, but everyone felt more confident about getting you well. However, my good feelings were short lived after your grandparents visited you. I never told you exactly what went on that day, but I feel the need to do so now.

Because I was so sleep deprived my fear about your

future grew. Would you live? Would you die? Would you suddenly stop walking, talking or remembering? I had no room for any more stress on my plate but the reality was I had to make immediate decisions concerning my job. As you recall, Katie, my job was working in a large psychiatric practice as the senior psychotherapist. It was a pretty big job, actually. I had many clients for whom I was responsible, I was in charge of the supervision, and I was the clinical coordinator who marketed the practice. Naturally your diagnosis demanded immediate changes in my work schedule.

I wanted to maintain balance in my work life and to be able to take care of you, our family and myself too. Since I had no previous experience with anything so immediate and traumatic that would compete with my job, I was uncertain about how to proceed. I bet you didn't know that I considered quitting altogether, did you, Katie? I did, but I thought that quitting might make you feel guilty and it could send you a bad message that I was falling apart. I also enjoyed my job and knew intuitively that an intellectual focus was good for my sanity. I really did not know what to do.

I decided to seek your grandfather's guidance. While retired, he had had a long professional career; I thought he could help me figure it out. During his visit with you in the hospital I told him my dilemma. While you talked to someone else who was visiting, he turned his head and lowered his voice so that only I could hear. "Well, Mary," he said, "it seems you care more about your clients than you do about your own daughter."

I stared at him, dumbfounded, sucker punched, and too stunned to speak. I glanced at you in the bed, so sweet with balloons all around. I bit my tongue; it would have been wrong to argue in front of you.   I'm sorry, Sweetheart, the story gets worse from here.

Your father and I left soon afterward; that was when I told him what happened. "Just let it go," he said. But you know me, Katie, I am not the kind of woman who can "just let it go" so I didn't. Your father's and my personality, our childhood histories of how we were raised, our individual fears for you, all of it exacerbated our differences. Your dad believes once it's done, it's done, one moves on and tries better the next time. I'm different. I need to make myself crystal clear when offended, hear an acknowledgement of the transgression and an apology when appropriate. It helps the sting of the injury and there is less chance the same problem will reoccur.

I decided to let it go but what I really did was shove my anger down.

That was a mistake, precious Katie, a humongous mistake.

Love,
Mom

chapter *Three*

*A "No" uttered from deepest conviction
is better and greater than a "Yes" merely uttered to please,
or what is worse, to avoid trouble.*

~MAHATMA GANDHI~

Holy inspirations arrive when we need them and my life over-
flows with them. Anyone who has a drop of Irish blood will always
look for the signs and wonders and often these gifts come in the
form of a real person. Let me back up in my story about Katie.
We were now ready to take her home following the first surgery.
Give yourself some time, the doctors told us, to process Katie's
options which were: one, get a second opinion or, two, begin chemotherapy and radiation treatments. We talked it over as a fam-

ily: Katie, Richard, Dick and me. Getting the second opinion was unanimous. Now I started bargaining with God.

I prayed, "If you let Katie live I promise I will do anything you want me to do. I will never complain about anything anymore. I will be a good wife, a wonderful person to everyone that I meet." No novena went unsaid. That is pretty typical in a situation such as ours. Dick stuck to the facts and called the most highly recommended pediatric neurosurgeon on the list, Dr. Fred Epstein, who asked us to send him all information, scans, and MRI's. Two days later Dr. Epstein called Dick back. "Mr. Brant," he said, "I have analyzed the before and after surgical MRI's and scans. I can do better. Please bring Katie up and let's talk about it."

Two days later we all drove to New York City. On Wednesday, July 12, 1989, Dr. Epstein (who asked to be called Fred) explained how he would remove as much of the remaining tumor as possible without damaging good brain tissue. "I won't paralyze you, Katie, and I think you should go for it." Katie looked pensive for a moment, smiled, and then gave Fred a grin and a thumb's up for a second surgery. Fred was that "holy inspiration" present in the flesh.

On July 20, Katie was again back in a hospital bed, only three weeks after her first surgery, but this time at New York University Hospital. A confident and smiling Dr. Epstein held her hand and assured her that all would be well. She did not seem afraid and even kidded him about his ostrich leather loafers and his green linen suit. He threw back his head, laughed and kissed her cheek, "Katie, I'll see you in the morning."

July 31, 1999
Dear Katie,

It took Dr. Epstein and his partner, Dr. Jeff Wisoff nine hours for your surgery. You were considerably sicker afterwards but on Day Four you felt well enough to sneak away, eat blueberry blintzes, drink Diet Cokes, and smooch with your new boyfriend, Chip, in the stairwell. Now it was time for a few visitors. The fourth day of your stay your grandparents again visited. I was quiet that day because I was still angry about what had never been addressed after your first surgery. And you know, Katie, that I won't be disingenuous and act nicey nice if that is not how I feel.

We again all stood next to your bed when your grandfather announced to everyone that he had a horrible sore throat. I stared at him. Was he joking? He must be joking. I felt incensed that he could jeopardize your fragile health so cavalierly. When your father and

I were alone your dad pleaded with me to again let it go, telling me I couldn't change his father. We argued about it again. Couples argue when they are upset, all couples. And I, like most people, reverted back to what I knew - my mother's adage that sometimes a little war is the only pathway for a little peace. Without further discussion with anyone, including your father, I began devising a plan of how to handle the volcano inside of me toward your grandfather. I also decided to keep my thoughts to myself.

The following day we gathered with Fred to discuss your aftercare and ready you for discharge from NYU Hospital. At the meeting you asked Dr. Epstein's permission to fly to Wolf, Wyoming. "I want to vacation with my boyfriend Chip's family!" Dr. Epstein tilted his head to the side as though he were processing his thoughts on fast forward. "All right, Katie, but no horseback riding!" When you looked over at us, your dad and I didn't know if you had a month to live or fifty years to live. But we saw the look on your face, Darling, and knew you would be happier going and safe with Chip's family so we said yes, too. Well, you went, had a ball, and disobeyed Fred and us by horseback riding every single day. Were we nuts to let you go? Was I mad at you for riding? We were and I was. But I respected your judgment to make choices for your own life's happiness.

Love,
Mom

After Katie returned from Wyoming, she needed additional rest and the immediate removal of four impacted wisdom teeth. (Dental procedures are necessary before starting chemotherapy because, once the chemo begins, the gum tissue cannot heal.) At this same time our Labrador retriever, unwell for months, took a turn for the worse and her kidneys began failing. It must have been August because I recall hearing the sonorous Katydids. So while Katie recovered from the removal of her wisdom teeth and two brain surgeries, our dog Beauty raised the bar on fidelity by rarely leaving her side.

~Looking Back Reflections ~

This discernment about whether Katie should go or not go out West was an example of places where as a parent I struggled with balancing my children's autonomy (so they could feel a strong sense of themselves) and my need for some peace of mind. I believe that struggle was overall a good thing because it offered me a chance to consider the places where I needed to be strict and the places I needed to ease up. As the children developed I tried my best to respect their own growing need for choice making.

One night Beauty couldn't stand anymore. That's when Dick and I retrieved an old camping comforter and placed her gingerly in it. Sling style, Dick at one end and me at the other, we carried our old dog to a quiet place, all 75 pounds of her, and placed her into another comforter. Weeping, I didn't know what we would do without such an integral part of our family. There are so many of us who have come to know the comfort a family pet brings. Those furry beasts and feathered friends walk through our lives with us through loss after loss, whether it is loss of a job, a marriage, a friend, or our health. Through challenge after challenge these animal companions help us make it through the night.

The next morning I rose early and hurried to check Beauty. Panting heavily, she looked up at me. I was beside myself, crying and calling out for St. Francis of Assisi to help her because during the night Dick and I had agreed to put her to sleep. Down on my knees, I stroked her head and whispered, "Beauty, I love you; we all do. You are such a good dog, such a loyal friend to all of us. I know you're not well and you're tired, so tired. It's okay for you to leave us, old girl." Beauty continued looking up at me and in that tiny moment, she was gone, just like that. My spirit sank as I petted her head for the last time. Than I ran in to tell Dick that Beauty had died. Shaking his head, he said it was time to dig her grave.

Clink, clink as the pick hit the rock, clink, clink. I ran to Richard's room where from under the mass of covers his seventeen-year old face peeked out, mummy like. "Riccchhhhhh," I said like Dickens's ghost from Christmas' past, "I'm sorry to wake you, but poor old Beauuuutttty diiiied. I'm sorry, Riccchhhhhh; you'll have to help your father digggg her grave."

"Oh Mom, no," he said.

"Oh Rich, yes," I said.

Downstairs I gathered Beauty's bowl, her leash and a handful of Kleenex, after which I composed a farewell letter to our family pet of twelve sweet years. The writer George Eliot (who was really Mary Ann Evans) once said, "We long for affection altogether ignorant of our faults. Heaven has accorded this to us in the uncritical canine attachment." That was how I felt about our dog Beauty: she was always glad to see me no matter what.

When all was in order, I walked into Katie's room and braced myself for tears. Her pretty face was swollen to dramatic proportions following the tooth extractions, her head had a big bald patch from her second surgery, and now dear Katie was crying about her constant companion dying. Outside, the four of us gathered around Beauty's grave like a sad scene out of *Angela's Ashes*. Dick, Richard and Katie wore sunglasses but not because it was sunny, because it wasn't. Dick stood erect with his hands on the shovel. I cleared my throat as I pulled out my letter. "Let's all say something to Beauty, I suggested.

"Oh Mom, no," Rich said.

"Oh Rich, yes," I replied.

I told our Beauty how glad we were that she had followed Richard home that day so long ago. I told her how naughty she was slipping away in the spring to roll around in our neighbor's horse manure. I read and sobbed the sentiments I believe we all held for our dog, who taught our children how to be gentle, how to be responsible. Yes, "The Beauts," as we called her, gave us many things over the years but that day our dog gave us her last gift - the gift of tears. Yes, Beauty's death allowed us all to cry, something that we had all pretty much held back on. And cry we did, all of us, for our Beauty, for ourselves, and for our dear Katie.

chapter *Four*

The Journey

One day you finally knew what you had to do, and began, though the voices around you kept shouting their bad advice – Though the whole house began to tremble and you felt the old tug at your ankles. *MEND MY LIFE!"each voice cried. But you didn't stop. You knew what you had to do, though the wind pried with its stiff fingers at the very Foundations – though their melancholy was terrible. It was already late enough, and a wild night and the road full of fallen branches and stones. But little by little, as you left their voices behind, the stars began to burn though the sheets of clouds, and there was a new voice, which you slowly recognized as your own, that kept you company as you strode deeper and deeper into the world, determined to do the only thing you could do -- determined to save the only life you could save.*

~MARY OLIVER~

Summer was now over. I avoided all contact with my husband's parents while we geared up for Katie's post surgery radiation and chemotherapy treatments. We did not know how she would manage the predictable exhaustion factor and attend her classes living away from us at Colgate University. Then an unexpected gift came. Katie applied and was accepted at The University of Pennsylvania. Yes, it was an Ivy League but this time I had nothing to do with Katie's choice. Her medical treatments would be accomplished at Children's Hospital and University of Pennsylvania Hospital right down the street.

The treatments were difficult and everyone's emotions were raw during this period. We all loved Katie so much and the thought of her going through this was overwhelming. Each of us felt the loss of our secure place in the world. When a family member we love is suffering the entire family is fractured. And remember, dear Reader, I was still sitting on my anger with my father-in-law. Anger, left unattended, does not just disappear, especially if it was not a one time event. No, it festers and it can take on a life of its own.

I decided I was now ready to put my anger behind me; decided to write a letter to my father-in-law describing exactly how I felt. It was an intense letter mincing no words. Days later the letter was returned and back in my mail box stamped "insufficient postage." I held the envelope like the bloody knife I knew it would become, grabbed some extra stamps, a larger envelope into which to put the first envelope, and took it personally to the post office. Days passed, weeks passed, no response came so I chose not to attend any family gatherings that year, including Christmas. That was when I told my husband about the letter. He would not go without me.

~Looking Back Reflections ~

There were so many decisions to make during this time. I prayed constantly for the wisdom to get it right. Looking back I think I could have used some time to de-stress even if it were some time to meet a friend for lunch or even talk on the telephone but I rarely did because I felt doing so would have made me a bad mother. I realize now that was "all or nothing thinking." Even on an airplane, when the oxygen mask drops down, the mother puts hers on first before putting it over the face of her child.

Long stressful months passed as Katie completed her lifetime's dose of radiation therapy and was a third of the way through her chemotherapy. Then one day, out of the blue, my secretary told me my father-in-law had called. I choose not to return it. A few days later a note arrived from my mother-in-law asking me to meet my father-in-law at a restaurant to talk with him, which I did. There he denied saying he did anything, told me I was intolerant, too sensitive, and that Dick and I spoiled our children. I told him he was right and that I would not tolerate his attempt to control me as he had everyone else in his life. I also told him that he was a bully and that I was not afraid of him. And those remarks, dear Reader, leveled the playing field forever.

Outside the restaurant the snowflakes fell. Walking to my car I felt reborn. For far too long I had allowed his defining of everyone in the family to define and confine me too. But I realized that after this day I would never project another father issue upon him again and I knew why: I didn't want him as a father anymore. I also recognized and owned my part in this ugly drama: my unfair personal projections onto a man who didn't want me as a daughter. Did that bother me? Yes, it absolutely did.

You see, dear Reader, when I first met my husband's family I was like Dumbo the Elephant after the crows gave him a feather which made him feel like he could magically fly. I just thought that he and everyone would like me and that I would have a nice older man to call dad. Lots of people project things like that onto other people. For me it was a fatherless adolescent's hope. My husband eventually helped me to understand that his father did not treat anyone affectionately and that I should not take it personally. But like Dumbo I finally got it and dropped the feather to test whether I could fly without the illusion; without the father complex. I discovered that I could.

When I finally got a little distance and flew above this murky situation, I realized that each of us had a role in this pas de deux. I believe it is difficult for any of us to face an action when we have been found out or when we ourselves know that our judgment was unfair, immature or mean spirited. In this case I believe that I was immature; he was mean-spirited. I kept trying to get something from him that I hadn't had enough of in my own childhood - a father. Withdraw-

> ~Looking Back Reflections ~
>
> *I realize now how conflicted was my desire to keep the peace between my spouse and his family and between my spouse and me. I realize now how much it cost me emotionally and the futility of it. Trying to please everyone pleased no one and it was connected to my childhood. Be the good girl; be the good boy. That thinking was inappropriate in adulthood.*

ing my own projections helped me realize that my father-in-law and I each shared the pride of the devil that day and many other days too, described perfectly by St. Thomas Moore who said, "The Devil never runs upon a man to seize him with his claws until he sees him on the ground, already having fallen by his own will." I know I am willful.

~Looking Back Reflections ~

I realize that it is unrealistic to think that communication patterns learned in childhood will change without introspection in adulthood. I think had I gotten myself into therapy earlier it could have diffused some of the negative energy which gripped me and I would have had some support and clarity to say "no" or "this far and no further" when I felt a personal boundary crossed. I also think I would have used the expression "The Third Party" when speaking about our marriage and my commitment to the marriage and desire for intimacy and that could have eased the power struggles that seemed about him or me winning the argument that underpinned our communication where his family of origin was concerned.

Hindsight is a marvelous teacher. Blessedly, time, introspection and distance from this situation clarified the complexities of this difficult period for me. I have now come to understand how my poor husband just wanted to fix the situation with Katie's health, period. He ignored the other circling problems with his parents because Katie's illness was his focus, trying to care for her, for us, go to work and have a life. Who can do it all on his or her own? Talk it out or act it out seemed the only two choices on my continuum, as I think they are for pretty much all of us. I wanted some help and resolution. The psychiatrist I worked for was psychologically unsophisticated and he referred me to an incompetent for couple therapy. I was so stressed out at this point I would have sat before a monkey. Several unproductive sessions later we realized that we had wasted our time and money with this nincompoop of a doctor so we quit the counseling - because there wasn't any. Exhaustion kept me from seeking another therapist who had a heart for the parents of a seriously ill child who had the skills to help us identify the dynamics of all the players involved in this unnecessary drama. Dick said, "Mare, we need to relax" and took it upon himself to buy a small second hand sailboat for us to play with instead.

Bobbing along in the bay, we discovered that I'm better at working the sails and Dick is better at working the tiller. We discovered that when I managed my feelings with less intensity, he expressed his with more.

I am a woman. Women feel sorrow deeply. Women focus on relationships. Women take longer to get to the point. Honestly, men become exhausted and distracted trying to listen to us when we go on and on. That would describe my husband and maybe yours, too. My husband is athletic and physical; he doesn't want to talk about his feelings all the time - many men are like that. Men can feel lost when huge stressors hit them. Find a compromise somewhere. You can do it; you can find it.

Talking on the boat was a great compromise for us. Where can you and your mate meet in the middle? Would your guy like to go to a movie or a ball game and talk afterwards with a beer and a burger? Playing is renewing. Playing is important. Playing renewed our original friendship which we now guard and cherish as Cerberus, the Greek three-headed dog monster guarded the cave of Persephone, the Queen of the Underworld.

I believe all of us can grow when we have insight. Maybe someday my in-laws will come to realize their mistakes as I reconsider mine. I confide that I do struggle with forgiving them. It is hard for me to pardon someone who has never admitted to any grievous wrongdoing, but maybe God will grant me the grace to actually do it someday no matter what they say or don't say. But either way I need to tell my truth to exorcise my own demons and to help other people struggling as we did.

We pushed ahead. Getting through the summer was hard, but as a family we made every necessary shift in our life, always putting Katie's recovery first. Because she herself had an indomitable spirit, she never stopped pursuing her dreams and her first dream was to have a normal college experience. And as I mentioned earlier, once Katie realized her treatments prevented her return to Colgate University for her sophomore year, she focused on living in Philadelphia and attending The University of Pennsylvania. This move went side-by-side with radiation treatments at The Hospital of University of Pennsylvania and chemotherapy treatments at Children's Hospital of Philadelphia.

Katie, as most kids her age, wanted to continue her young adult independence and didn't want to be deprived of it because of a cancer diagnosis. "Mom and Dad please don't say no to my living at the Kappa Alpha Theta Sorority House!" Another tough decision for Dick and me and we weighed it carefully. "Two surgeries, forty-five days of radiation, thirteen and a half months of chemotherapy and a sorority house, Katie?"

"It's my life, why would I take chances with my health!" Here again the letting go motif presented to Dick and me. The letting go of securities and illusions that we can control our lives if we are cautious. So that autumn semester Katie lived where she wanted, attended all of her classes and found some time with her boyfriend Chip to volunteer at The Ronald

McDonald House downtown. He also went to every radiation treatment with Katie while pursuing his own double major at Penn. They were an amazing young couple. Katie Brant was living her life; she was unstoppable.

August 2, 1999
Dear Katie,

Saying yes to your living at Penn was tough for your dad and me. It came down to balancing your desire for autonomy with our need to protect you. When we relaxed a little we realized that any plan was reversible. Flexibility, not rigidity, works so much better with raising children, and you were gloriously happy when we said yes. That reality, then and now, Katie, is an enormous comfort to us.

Love,
Mom

chapter *Five*

Our children "are the sons and daughters
of Life's longing for itself."

~KAHLIL GIBRAN~

At The University of Pennsylvania, despite her cancer surgeries, radiation therapies, and chemotherapies, Katie's Colgate
sorority transferred her into Penn's sister sorority house and she
was soon awarded a Benjamin Franklin Scholarship for academic excellence. In addition to attending her regular scheduled
classes, Katie additionally enrolled in an elective course at Penn's
Medical College on brain tumors. She did this for one reason
only: she wanted to research her own tumor.

In the class handouts, papers and text books, Jonathan Finlay, M.D. was regularly cited in reference to her type of tumor, so off to New York Katie went to meet this top-notch oncologist/ hematologist in the field of pediatric cancers.

Dr. Finlay was as charmed by Katie as she was by him and that very day he agreed to be her doctor of record, hired her as an assistant for that coming summer to gather and analyze statistics on a new children's chemotherapy protocol, and arranged for Katie to reside at a local YWCA. She was ecstatic about these windfalls: living in The Big Apple, earning college credits for her research, engaging an exceptionally gifted doctor who became her friend, and getting published in a major medical journal to boot. Alongside of these accomplishments, chemotherapy and radiation therapy, Katie graduated on time and with honors.

A gigantic celebration party followed where we transported two full yellow school busses of graduates from Penn's campus in Philadelphia to our home in Valley Forge. We also added a supplemental graduation gift: backpacking through Europe with two girlfriends for six weeks. This was a requested present and we nervously agreed to her wanderlust. Katie sent us many colorful and outrageous post cards over those forty plus days calling frequently with her excitement, laughter and wild stories. Her father and I suspected that with three beautiful women prancing through the Continent, there were probably many 'untold' stories as well.

Upon Katie's return she accepted a position with Saks Fifth Avenue. Her dad and I were not sure what an "intellectual history major" wanted with a "buyer training program in retail" but Katie's dream was to live in New York City; retail was simply a means to an end. Surgery, however, left Katie with a handicap: she could not remember new faces. When someone said, "Did you receive those reports yet, Katie?" She didn't know who had even asked.

August 5, 1999
Dear Katie,

Oh, those small miracles along your path that The Good God tossed as gold coins. Like that lovely young doctor you met on the train, the one who understood your situation and finally named it, "prosopagnosia," or "face blindness." You were so relieved! He went on to say that temporal lobe surgery sometimes causes this condition, then handed you the name of the doctor under whom he had personally studied! Because your surgeries were well documented, this world-renowned Doctor Antonio Demassio and his wife, Dr. Hanna Demassio, flew you out to The University of Iowa for extensive testing of your facial memory capabilities thereby assisting their clinical research and you, too. But you went more for the research benefits because contributing to a larger cause that benefited suffering children in the world always met with your generous response, "How can I help?" even if it meant giving up your vacation, which you did that year.

Paying attention to what you needed always worked for you, Katie. You attracted the right people all the time. You paid attention to the synchronicities as confirmations from God and somehow found comfort and meaning in your suffering. You did it consciously too, Katie, and with a brave heart, by demonstrating to everyone that suffering does not destroy the joy of a person who is joyful by nature.

You also did it the old fashioned way: simply by being yourself.

Love,
Mom

*Artemis as goddess of the hunt and goddess of the moon
was a personification of an independent feminine spirit.
The archetype she represents enables a woman to seek her
own goals on terrain of her own choosing.*

~JEAN SHINODA BOLEN, M.D.~
*GODDESSES IN EVERY WOMAN:
A NEW PSYCHOLOGY OF WOMEN*

Katie's regular MRI's showed that her tumor had gone into remission and Katie believed her illness was history. I wasn't completely convinced, but as an Artemis mother I worked diligently to sublimate my maternal anxiety because I wanted Katie to live her life in a large unrestrained fashion, and worrying about me would have killed her faster than any cancer would have.

August 10, 1999
Dear Katie,

We identified with the Artemis archetype, believing her independent and courageous nature mirrored our own. The Romans called her Diana; religious history called her Joan of Arc, and I just called her Katie. I loved your fortitude, Katie. I loved how you wouldn't allow anything to stop you. You were determined, a leader; you loved children and the causes of women! Validating you and highlighting your strengths was exhilarating for me. With your highly extroverted temperament you thrived on people, adventure and good works while your radiant and unrestrained nature propelled you forward your entire life.

So even while this mother of yours felt nervous about your backpacking around Switzerland, Italy,

Spain, and England, I borrowed that famous line from Rocky Balboa, "KATIE, GO FOR IT!" When you called me from a phone booth on Fifth Avenue crying about your narcissistic wacko boss and asked for my input about quitting that first job, I said, "KATIE, GO FOR IT!"

~Looking Back Reflections ~

I realize in hindsight how Katie pursued her dreams and aspirations with a dogged determination. I admired that so much and I wanted to champion her to reach her goals. I have also come to realize how much I like it when someone encourages me and tells me that I can do it; that I can throw my rope around the moon and make it mine.

Now when I speak and pray to you in my heart about writing this book, asking you for your advice, I hear you tell me, "MOM, GO FOR IT."

Love,
Mom

*"Today I thought about all of the children I
have met over the years. I thought about their scars,
their baldness, their fragility, their families and all of their
bravery....Without a shadow of a doubt,
I know why I survived...."*

~KATIE BRANT, IN PARIS, NOV. 1, 1994~

That quote was part of a letter that Katie sent to her dad and me from Paris, on All Saint's Day and five years post surgery. It's clear how affected she was by the suffering of little children. After Katie quit her job at Saks, enrolled in a six-week language school in Paris then found a French family to live with, she called me. "Mom, I need to make time for myself just to think. Do you think Dad will be okay with my decision?"

"Katie," I said, "Do what you need to do. Your father will understand that you need to do this."

As the fog burned off those early Parisian mornings, Katie Brant peddled down the Champs-Elysees, fresh croissant in hand, smile of gratitude on her face and a prayer in her heart. These daily delights supplemented her regular routine visits to Sacre-Coeur Basilica and Notre Dame Cathedral for personal reflection and long talks with God about her passions, her dreams, her health and her future.

August 14, 1999
Dear Katie,

You wrote that returning to Paris felt so powerful; that you knew God was calling you for a deeper purpose that you could no longer deny. I believe that, darling

Katie. You mentioned that before leaving New York, you spoke with Dr. Finlay specifically about raising money for pediatric brain tumors. You said you wrote separate letters to Doctors Finlay, Wisoff and Epstein from Paris about a calling you believed you had not yet answered.

> *"I know why I survived.... I need to see this new foundation happen... I have never been so sure of anything in my entire life. When I was first diagnosed, I bargained with God. I said that if He let me keep it (my life) I would not waste it. I would make a difference. Yes, I am nervous, but at a deeper level I feel so much better."*

I picture you sitting there writing that important letter to them, to us and to yourself, really. I picture you basking in the possibilities. I picture you in that moment when you knew the direction in which you were headed and the great joy you must have felt! You know, Katie, when your dad and I finished reading your letter we smiled at one another. "Well Dick," I laughed, "it looks like our Katie's got a plan unfolding." And your dad? Well, he just kept smiling that Dick smile.

Love,
Mom

It was always emotionally difficult for me to let Katie leave after her initial diagnosis. I just worried about her. I often wonder would I have felt that degree of concern had she never been ill. Certainly separation from our children and loved ones is an ongoing, lifelong process. When Katie and Richard left for nursery school, then kindergarten, Dick and I were introduced to 'the leaving.' Grammar school, overnight camp and high school followed, then college, jobs, an apartment and living in another state. All this leaving challenges the original dynamic of a family because suddenly the day of departure has arrived. When the time comes for the final launch, when the young adult child begins the separation, the autonomy of living his or her own life, many mothers feel that their job is over. "My baby is leaving and I'm falling apart at the seams!"

I felt like that; I'm no different from other mothers. We moms love hanging out with our kids and their friends, cooking, laughing and making a family life. It is a wonder and a blessing beyond belief. The fun, the gaiety; we're not sure what we'll do in their absence. It's beyond hard letting them go, but remember we gave them wings; now we must let them fly.

August 21, 1999
Dear Katie,

Your surgeries and treatments regularly altered your plans and forced your return home many, many times. Reminds me about that question, "Do you want to hear God laugh? Tell Him your plans." Your brother Richard also returned home the summer after his graduation from Dickinson College. Trying to find meaningful employment is typical of the newly graduated, but when a financial crunch hits and living with mom and pop looks inevitable, I think most young adults feel like life has slammed them.

When your dad and I moved to Connecticut during your brother's last year of college, Rich asked us if we had chosen our home as part of a witness protection program, to which we laughed and responded, "Of course." But things turned serious one morning when Richard stood on the back stairs. "Mom, I can't figure out who I am and what my life is about while living here with you and dad again." My heart skipped a beat when I heard your brother's words. We stared at one another a long minute as I felt the mother ship begin to shake, begin to split off. Inhaling a deep breath I placed my hand over his hand on the banister.

"Then Rich," I said, "Go and find out who you are and what you are about." Trust me, Katie, I wanted to keep you and your brother close to me forever but I knew this was the music of Ulysses' Sirens. I put my needs aside knowing it would have been selfish and neurotic not to. A few days later Richard walked into the family room, "Mom, Dad, I'm leaving this Podunk of a town." There was such playfulness and tenderness in his voice, so typical of your brother. "Hey," I responded, "no way this is a Podunk town!" Then he has me in a headlock laughing. "So where are you heading to, Rich?"

"Southern Cal-I-FOR-NI-A - and I'm leaving in uno, dos, tres days." He had no job and little money but your dad and I had more faith in our hearts than apprehension about your brother's capabilities but before either of us could respond and tell him so, Richard added, "And, Mom and Pop, Caroline's going with me!" We were speechless. But your brother was an adult now and somewhere deep within us we believed the cross country trip would be life changing for him in a positive way. We also thought it would more than likely lead toward Richard making Caroline his life's partner. "We'll get jobs, not to worry, Mom and Dad!" So we trusted and we let go.

Yes, Katie, somehow we mothers and fathers can

let go. Somehow we parents can stop focusing on the time apart. Somehow we moms and dads can survive our children leaving us.

Love,
Mom

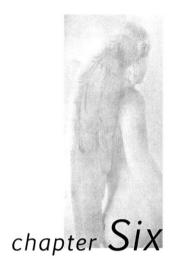

chapter *Six*

*"There was never a place for her in the ranks of
the terrible, slow army of the cautious.
She ran ahead where there were no paths."*

~DOROTHY PARKER~
WRITING ABOUT ISADORA DUNCAN

Some people take a breath between strokes. Not Katie. After her return from Paris she looked for another job. In no time she was hired by Time, Inc. in Manhattan. Katie was psyched. On her personal time she researched cause-related marketing and moved to an adorable apartment in Greenwich Village with her dear friend Madeline and vacationed in Kennebunkport, Maine and the Hamptons on Long Island. Yes, dear Katie was well, happy and living large so you can imagine my joy, dear Reader.

During this time my mother discovered a lump in her lower abdomen. Her fate was sealed by the head nephrologist at Memorial Sloan-Kettering Hospital who confided to all of us, "Cancerous kidney, Mrs. Hurley, and it is metastasized. Truthfully, I wouldn't recommend surgery under these conditions."

My mother, always courageous, asked immediately, "How long do I have, Doctor?"

"Probably three months, Mrs. Hurley; I'm sorry."

"Mary Jane and Dick, please take me back to Collingswood; I want to be in my own house and you can stay with me there."

"Sure, Mom," I responded, "but how about we wait until you feel a little better? What do you say that we go back to our home in Connecticut for awhile, Dick will pour you a lovely glass of wine and we'll watch a great movie?" And so we did, movie after movie, while I held Mom's hand on our comfortable couch and watched the days and Mother slip away.

Every morning, before Dick left for work, he would comment about her bathrobe. "Well, Mom, is it the pink one or the blue one today?" I thought it so sweet, this little interaction between them. After the exchange I would crawl into Mom's bed, take her hand, and listen to her tell me about her life and all the people in it. This was Mom's pilgrimage coming to closure. This was Mom's making peace with her entire world. People in my profession call it a life review and it is an important part of one's journey. It was a very special time for me and also for Mom, who was open and sweet and loving.

Erik Erikson, known for his study of ego development, called this final time in a person's life, the eighth stage, "Integrity versus Despair."

My mother died as she lived: with great integrity. She gave the three of us kids a pretty good upbringing, not perfect, but good. We were her contribution to this world. Mom was fiercely independent, stayed vigorous and never compromised herself for anyone. What one told her stayed with her and she never betrayed a confidence. Mom modeled courage to me more than anyone I had ever known besides

~Looking Back Reflections ~

Having lost many people close to me and worked in hospice many years I am actively trying to live my life with Erikson's model in mind which simply means not to betray my ideal self and when I fail and miss the mark to quickly find the right path again.

Katie. She was also practical and stoic, mature and grounded. By that I mean Mom saw things and situations as they were, not bigger or smaller. Neither did she get really depressed or gleeful either. And while she wasn't a joker, she had a wonderful sense of the absurd.

Seriously, mom could be funny as hell sometimes. Once when she was highly medicated and on some bad drug, she told

Dick and me that she heard a priest singing under her window and that rosary beads were hanging from the ceiling. I thought, "Oh no, Jesus is sending a sign and Mom's leaving tonight!" But Mom didn't die that night. She left this world from my brother Frank's home where he and his wife Chris took care of her during her final month of life, something that they both wanted to do. Mom took her final breath alone when Frank left her room for some water. I told him it was okay because our mother, Jane Elizabeth McCart Hurley, was private and that was how she wanted it.

It was devastating losing my mother, almost three months to the day from her diagnosis. My brother said she would live to be a hundred - he was off by twenty-one years. Reflecting upon Mom's life, it made sense to me that her life was about Catholic images. Rosary beads hanging from the ceiling was real to her because her faith was real to her. But it was beyond sad when she was with me, weak and tired and saying once a day, "It's better not to know, Mary Jane." I would give her a hug and repeat, "It's better not to know, Mom?" And she would nod her head and sigh. It simply broke my heart in two.

Yes, Mom gave us everything she could. She had a life that was hard, lonely and sad. Looking at pictures of my father and her together I could see how his leaving made her such a different woman. She was happy when he was here. Mom was also the only parent I had known since I was thirteen years old. She was wise, deeply religious, and I loved her. Hemingway once wrote that the world breaks everyone and afterward some are strong at the broken places. That describes my mother perfectly.

~Looking Back Reflections ~

I have come to understand that even when parents love their children they sometimes hurt them just by being who they are. I have also come to realize that even when we love our parents we sometimes hurt them just by being who we are.

In the aftermath of a parent's death there is work to be done: furniture and clothes to donate to the poor, papers, photographs and personal belongings to sort through. Frank and I did the physical sorting and discarding in a huge dumpster. He also listed mom's house for sale - the house she had lived in since she was nine months old. I chose the paperwork detail, hoping to uncover some clue about our father's emotional health, any piece of information shedding light upon his suicide because clearly my father's self-inflicted death was a trauma I needed to understand. So like an old hound dog I rummaged and sniffed around our attic in the middle of August for five uninterrupted hours, temperature an insufferable 102 degrees, looking for anything to give me closure. What did I discover? Nada.

Our sister, Eileen, made like a ghost during mom's illness - it was simply too much for her constitution - fragile since childhood - and Mom's cancer diagnosis didn't help. Her son Eric took up much of her time so that was also a contributing factor. Nevertheless, I felt mixed about Eileen's absence because I knew she loved our mother and I felt she would live to regret avoiding those last months. On the other hand, a person's psyche can take just so many hits, and Eileen's emotional bankruptcy, after her own neck cancer and her darling Jennifer's long illness and death, must have left little resources for any more emotional withdrawals. But every choice has its cost and its consequences and everyone lives with some regret. I think my sister does now have regrets and I think that can be a terrible place of no return.

As the days passed after Mom's death I began to feel jittery, began to feel on alert as if a rapist lurked behind every bush. I also felt like an orphan because, quite frankly, I was one. I've heard many clients express that same feeling when their last parent died. It is an odd, lonely, desert-like experience.

One night, eleven weeks after my mother's funeral, my husband stood visibly agitated in our kitchen. "What's wrong, Dick?" He offered no response.

I moved back defensively and shouted, "DON'T TELL ME SOMETHING IS WRONG WITH KATIE!"

He reached for my hand, "Mare, the tumor is back. Whatever it takes, we'll figure out what to do."

August 24, 1999
Dear Katie,

You were symptom free for 3 1/2 beautiful years. My God, a dormant cancer is meaner and more aggressive than a junkyard dog. These cancers also get more drug resistant over time. Precious Girl, how could you bear hearing the dreadful word "Cancer" again? Your third brain surgery commenced on October 25, 1995. And while you felt our angst, we felt your hope. You repeated over and over, "I'll be fine, just fine; God isn't done with me yet."

Recuperating in the hospital you laughed and commented about your Time Inc. bosses and co-workers. "Wasn't it hilarious seeing Deanna and E.B. rally with my Time friends wearing those crazy brain hats, Mom?" Twenty something humor, I chuckled to myself. When they handed you that emerald green baseball cap with 'Lucky' embroidered on it I thought, lucky? I was grateful you could still walk, talk, and smile. But you, outrageous Katie, laughed and plunked the cap on your bandaged, shaved head.

After leaving NYU Hospital we happily headed back to Ridgefield, Connecticut. Crossing the Triborough Bridge you sighed and smiled at me, "Isn't the view gorgeous, Mom?" Together we watched the gulls soar and swoop overhead on this beautiful sunny day. I opened the window, invited the soft breezes in as I reached for your hand. Allowing the love we shared to wash over us, I accepted another chance to prepare your favorite foods, play board games and get you back into your game. "Can we pick up hoagies and chips for lunch today, Mom?"

"Of course, dear Heart, anything you want. Anything your heart desires."

Love,
Mom

After Katie's third surgery, we played Scrabble twice daily, minimally. In between word challenges she formulated ideas for cause-related marketing and lined up her contacts by phone. As I listened to Katie make conference call after conference call, verbalizing how she was going to help little kids, it amazed me how little she worried about her own brain tumors. I suppose that was because she was too busy making the world a better place when she wasn't beating the pants off of me in Scrabble.

August 26, 1999
Dear Katie,

Your surgeon and friend, Jeff Wisoff, M.D., said you did not possess one ounce of self-pity. I knew that; you rarely thought about your own cancer outside of finding a cure or a better chemotherapy. Your interest in pursuing ideas was fascinating, Sweetheart; I loved listening to them develop. Besides, I knew my attention to your causes made you happy and I wanted to make you happy.

Being together made me happy. Being together made you happy. We tried making one another happy.

Love,
Mom

Some of Katie's Penn friends had moved to New York City and Caryn Karmatz-Rudy, a Kappa Alpha Theta sister, was one. Caryn was also a senior editor with Warner Books then so when Katie returned to work after her month's recuperation, she called Caryn and asked if she could meet one of Caryn's authors: Sarah Ban Breathnach, writer of the New York Times best seller, *Simple Abundance.* "Of course!" Caryn said. So Katie, with all of her hope and ambitions, went to the public appearance event where Sarah was speaking. A simple "hello and how do you do" just wasn't enough for Katie. She needed an up close and personal connection, so she hustled when Sarah exited and waved for the taxi. "Do you mind us sharing a cab back to Warner, Sarah? I would really like to speak with you about something important."

In that brief taxi ride, Katie explained to Sarah her ideas for cause-related marketing. Sarah asked her straight out, "Katie, what can I do to help you?"

"Sarah, I would like you to introduce me to the Chairman of Time Warner Trade Publishing, Larry Kirshbaum."

August 28, 1999
Dear Katie,

I loved when you called, breathless and excited about your meetings with Larry; sharing how Sarah made it happen and how delighted Larry felt about your start-up ad campaign with an approved cause-related marketing component. I always ran to tell your father who would smile, shake his head, and ask, "How does she do it, Mare?" Hey, it's no secret if you ask me. You did it because you were beautiful, you were smart, and you had moxie, charm and good ideas; that's how you did it.

Love,
Mom

Katie was incredibly outgoing and other-centered. When she focused on someone, they felt special and loved. It's about generosity and Katie clearly shared St. Ignatius Loyola's spirit there because she was generous with her time, her money and her affections. Katie never understood a miserly spirit; why anyone would be stingy with their compliments, their concern, or their feelings and, quite frankly, neither can I.

August 31, 1999
Dear Katie,

You affirmed every friend, every doctor, every nurse, every family member and every little cancer patient you ever met. You were loved by so many, Katie B., and not just because you were so loveable, but because you loved so well.

Deepak Chopra was right when he said, "Give what you want to get."

Love,
Mom

Katie was once again in rhythm with New York City: working, playing, living her life but sadly, seven months after that third surgery and recuperation, she required a fourth. Devastated, we couldn't understand how our daughter could look so healthy, beautiful, be dating, having fun, and then relapse. Katie wanted to be cancer free; she had the surgery. On recuperative day nine, her vision was severely blurred and compromised. Because it was a weekend I dialed the doctor on call and suggested that Katie's medication might be a problem and could he please test her blood. He was dismissive and condescending, "What are you, a nurse?"

My unrelenting urging and my response that I had cared for Katie for many years convinced him to reluctantly fax a prescription for a blood test to be drawn at our local hospital. Four hours later he called to report the results, "Indeed, Mrs. Brant, Katie's blood has reached toxic levels; it seems she was overmedicated." I threw my chances for sainthood right out the window, along with humility.

"Now do you mind faxing in that prescription, Doctor?"

September 2, 1999
Dear Katie,

Sometimes mothers have to be tough, have to be assertive. Assertive people get their needs met by being honest and direct. People feel secure in their presence. Aggressive people get their needs met, too, but usually at another's expense, hands around the throat bullying and no one really likes them. And passive people? Their shoulder shrugging simply exhausts everyone, then they'll make a passive-aggressive move, everyone else feels mad and just wants them to go away. But, Sweetheart, we put that smug doctor's attitude to bed and got on with life by heading to Long Beach Island, New Jersey, for two more weeks of recuperation. Seagulls gliding, waves roaring and friends dropping by for a game of chess and a beer seemed the best remedy of all for you, Katie.

But my God, that last weekend when you said you wanted to go night fishing, I tried offering you every rational argument to dissuade you! The thought of you out on the high sea in a rocking, smelly, party fishing boat in the dark with a bunch of strange men made me a complete wreck. But you kept insisting that you wanted

to go, telling me fishing was a relaxing sport, no matter
how many times I asked, "Are you sure it's about relaxing, and not about that young captain, the one with the
killer tan?"

But you just smiled, winked, and gave my cheek a
little kiss.

Love,
Mom

After her recuperation at the beach, Katie returned to
New York City. She wanted to be well and being pro-active,
she arranged a meeting with Dr. Finlay concerning her relapses. "Katie, your regular chemotherapies just aren't formidable
enough for controlling the tumor's growth. I'm strongly rec-
ommending a stem cell transplant. It's a harsh procedure and it
will take months to complete," Dr. Finlay said. He described it as
a sophisticated, blood separating process. He explained that the
hematopoietic stem cells, or immature cells, develop into the full
range of blood cells in our body. They originate from the bone
marrow but are found (under normal circumstances) in smaller
numbers in the circulating blood. These stem cells are removed
by a machine in a process called harvesting. Then these cells are
immediately frozen.[2]

---

2 Memorial-Sloan Kettering Hospital Website

Next, the patient receives mega doses of chemotherapy to kill the cancer. These potent drugs cause the patient's blood counts to fall dangerously low. Yes, dear Reader, the procedures can be life threatening. The final step is replacing the patient's original baby (stem) cells back into his or her body, usually through a Broviac, and these returned cells then rejuvenate new healthy cell growth.

September 5, 1999
Dear Katie,

Jonathan Finlay had a plan to manage your chronic tumors. It offered hope. At the second meeting, after he explained the harshness of a stem cell transplant, you responded, "I want to do it."

"KT," Jonathan said, "during your treatment you will need to stay in close proximity to the hospital, not your apartment in the Village; it's simply too far away." Emphatically, he added, "and you can't do this without help," glancing over at your father and me. That was a head's up for us that this was going to be difficult, very difficult.

"Are you with me Mom and Dad?" you asked.

"Forever, Katie," we responded.

That same day I found a small apartment near Memorial Sloan-Kettering Hospital. Three days later we came into New York City by train from Katonah, New York. At Memorial Sloan-Kettering your stem cells were harvested and your arm blew up to an enormous and painful degree. It made you cry. That weekend we moved our things into the apartment; the next day the stem cell hospitalization began.

During your first three months, you threw up ninety-three consecutive days. Your beautiful eyes rarely looked normal: pupils dilated one minute and pin points the next. You had minimal energy to speak; less to walk. The stem cell transplant was undoubtedly the single most awful thing that I have ever seen a human being endure, never mind that you were the one suffering it, Katie. One afternoon you whispered, "Mom, why don't you go and have a nice meal and a drink and see a Broadway show tonight." I kissed you, said I would think about it, but honestly? Hitting Broadway after a nice dinner was the last thing I wanted to do. Getting you through this ordeal, followed by my staying sane were my only objectives.

The stem cell procedure was so radical it could have killed you; it almost did for God's sake and it almost killed me. The days were long, sickness was everywhere. Finally your counts plummeted and it was time then for the return of your stem cells. The medical professionals entered your room, nodded respectfully at you, then at me. When the in-charge nurse's serene eyes met mine I swear I felt God's presence, Katie, because I experienced the deepest secret of my own heart: that the transplant would be successful. When the nurse turned to leave the room, she looked back and smiled at me the way a mother smiles at another mother.

For weeks following the treatment, you were unbearably weak and sick. Because you had no immunity to fight infection, I discouraged all visitors except a few of your intimate friends. Rich and Caroline were still living in California and visited when they could but they never missed calling you every day. When you spoke on the phone to them, or anyone, you were always so cheerful that your illness stayed your secret domain. Because no one saw you, no one had a clue about how thin and fragile you really were and that's how you wanted it. I stayed out of it, saying nothing unless pushed. Besides, no one really likes talking about illness, that's just the way it is. But because Katie's body became exceedingly more fragile during the stem cell procedure, her doctors agreed to divide her dose into two transplants.

Your suffering was intense and it made me think about Jesus, Katie. It made me remember that Jesus had to do what He had to do: accept and meet his fate. I'm consoled reflecting on that thought because it reminds me that even in our darkest hours we are not walking on virgin ground. Broken bodies ravaged by illness, or minds tortured by despair can find a comfort knowing that a great and extreme suffering has occurred before. That thought gave me courage. That thought reminded me to trust God had a plan. That thought connected me to everyone everywhere who was suffering because the human condition is a place where we are undeniably all one.

The famous first president of the Czech Republic, Vaclav Havel, once said that hope is an orientation of the spirit, an orientation of the heart. It is not the conviction that something will turn out well, but the certainty that something makes sense, regardless of how it turns out. Your illness, dear Katie, prompted years of uncertainty with no guarantee that your circumstances would end favorably. Nevertheless, we all stayed hopeful and we all stayed courageous. You were our role-model for courage. You and I told each other that this was a race for wellness, a marathon. So like Lance Armstrong, we stayed focused; like Tiger Woods, we stayed in the zone, and like great athletes, we expected to win.

I'm crying now, precious Katie, remembering all of this. You were such a strategic thinker, such a big picture person. You kept your eye on the goal; I took the job as your coach. "We can do it, Katie," I said to you over and over. "We can do it, Mom," you always answered back. Now in my heart I still say we did it, darling Girl, and we made some people pretty happy along the way, especially you and me.

Love,
Mom

Katie and I accepted the present moment. We accepted our journey right where we were. I took Katie's lead here. She was the first light always. St. Catherine of Siena once said that to the true servant of God, every place is the right place; every time is the right time. Accepting life that way makes it a little less rough, not easy, just less of a struggle. Katie and I both believed that if one is not spiritually well, then they shall never really be well. Our relationship was sweet and easy because we consciously chose the spiritual path to sustain and guide us regardless of the outcome. We also made the conscious choice never to go down the "what if" street, always guarding our thoughts, feelings and behaviors because we knew that neither one of us would have recovered if either of our moods sunk.

Depression is contagious and I had already had one episode, but you know what, dear Reader? Joy is contagious also. So it was within that construct of joy that our whole family sought to maintain buoyant spirits. That may sound peculiar given the seriousness of Katie's circumstances. But honestly, dear Reader? It was easy being cheerful around Katie; she was like the 4th of July.

September 9, 1999
Dear Katie,

How your father managed the drive into Manhattan every night from his job in Pleasantville, New York, bringing us kisses and his dry humor, I'll never know. He never failed to ask about our day and I explained the routine: be at the hospital by 10:00 a.m.; depart by 6:00 p.m. Sometimes you walked; sometimes I brought you in a wheel-chair. After you registered yourself at the front desk, a nurse weighed you in, blood tests were taken and monitored, treatments were administered accordingly and a mad scramble for chairs and beds for patients and caregivers commenced.

Your tumor was classified as a pediatric tumor because you were diagnosed at eighteen. Jonathan Finlay was a pediatric oncologist and hematologist and he wanted to treat you in the children's unit even though now you were a young adult. The pediatric floor itself was small, cramped and overflowing with sick, screaming children - many of whom underwent regularly scheduled spinal taps. As a young mother I never had to bear such suffering, such bone chilling anxiety. The clinic was worse than any Boris Karloff movie, a real Pit and The Pendulum with a sensate deprivation on the one hand and total sensory overload on the other. As you know, Katie, I am particularly sensitive to sounds, visual stimuli and odors: the deafening noise levels of teenagers listening to music and watching the TV's -that were always turned up way too loud - drove me bonkers. After three months, we both had heard enough talk shows, Bugs Bunny, MTV and soap operas to last ten lifetimes.

Young children, who didn't know they were sick with cancer, ran around with their little bald heads and sallow chemo faces while their other siblings joined them in the tag because many parents simply lacked options for extra childcare. Often families drove as long as three hours, then returned home every day because they had to get back to their other children. Finding or being able to afford babysitters so frequently added to their daily stresses.

The greasy odors of chicken, hamburgers, french fries and fish sticks grossed me out, ugh, but for you it was worse - the smells made you nauseous so periodically you announced authoritatively, "No more food allowed in the treatment areas!" Many moms, worn out from daily stress, ate continuously. Glazed eyes from food comas and accompanying weight gains were understandably common. Some women, the more hyper types like your mother, became pencil thin instead. It was about control for all of us really. What went into our mouths was the only thing that we could control.

Many children were on steroids - a drug which prompted ferocious appetites and resulted in colossal weight gains. These little kids' appearances were altered so dramatically that they didn't even look like kids anymore. The typical adolescents were keenly aware they had cancer and most were quiet and withdrawn. Concern with physical appearance at that age is fierce enough in normal development, so we were sensitive to the teen with no hair, no eyebrows and no great high school dance to look forward to. It was heartbreaking for us to see day after day, wasn't it, Sweetheart?

Initially many mothers thought you were a mother because the majority of the children were so young. "Where's your child?" newcomers would ask you. "I am the child!" you responded with a chuckle. When you needed space I took a walk or lit a candle at Mother Elizabeth Seton's Church the patron Saint of Caretakers. On days that you slept, I sat quietly next to you and read, especially Clarissa Pinkola Estes book, *Women Who Run with the Wolves.*

Women seeking a cure for their child came to Memorial Sloan-Kettering from the world over: the US, China, Israel, India, Japan, Greece, Africa, and Saudi Arabia just to name a few countries. The horror stories of pediatrics elsewhere in the world gave us a new appreciation of the United States. These moms sometimes traveled alone with their sick child while the fathers stayed home, sometimes in another country, to be with their other children whom this mother might not see nor hug and hold again for months. More often than not moms spoke only in their native tongue, but universally we mothers all shared a common tongue and bond: we knew our children could die. While a crushing possibility for sure, it never allowed room for pity because courage and patience were the virtues admired here and most everyone had them.

Many dads, like yours, came at the end of long workdays. When kids are little and sick, they usually just want their mommies so we saw many more mothers and grandmothers. One couple, the man and a woman each twenty-four years old, had two children being treated for two different cancers: one eighteen months; one five years old. As Katie frequently said someone always had it worse. Yes, the days were long and difficult but with the exception of your father I wouldn't have asked anyone to take my place because, selfishly, I wanted that privilege. You see, dear Katie, you and I didn't just love one another; we liked one another's company. The "compatibility thing" was the "heart thing" that caught our soul's attention, every single time.

Love,

Mom

~Looking Back Reflections ~

I learned a few powerful coping strategies while in the hospital with Katie. She even named them. The first was "Chosen Denial" meaning that while we were cognizant of her serious cancer status, we didn't live there every emotional minute. A second we called "Distraction" meaning we played with the children, talked to the parents, or played Scrabble with each other. A third we called "Focus" meaning we implemented powerful and hopeful thoughts like getting Katie well and planning for upcoming holidays and celebrations: a focus on the future. But the most important one was "Gratitude". Katie prompted me every night with the latter.

"Mom, did you make up your gratitude list yet?" It was hard for me in the beginning but I figured if Katie could find something to be grateful for, couldn't I? Well, I first began with being grateful that my health was so good because if I became sick, who would take care of Katie? I never even had a sniffle.

Each day she had to cross a terrible chasm,
a bottomless hole of not knowing
what to hope or believe.

~AMY TAN~
THE OPPOSITE OF FATE

Katie's life, from the age of eighteen on, was a trust walk. Despite everything she had to hear and endure, she did not act fearful. She did not panic. During this period we kept our spirits elevated, our thoughts optimistic. We believed a positive attitude had its own rewards.

We also believed it was a choice.

September 12, 1999
Dear Katie,

Early in the game you and I agreed this battle would be long and arduous. We asked one another, "How do we want to be perceived?" We answered, "Joyful!" Some days were very hard for me, Katie, because on the one hand I was deeply worried about you but on the other hand I knew you needed me to stay strong and optimistic. For years I have taught many clients about practicing positive goals. When you and I practiced joy as our positive goal every day, it became as natural as breathing in and breathing out.

Love,
Mom

Days before Christmas, 1997, the first transplant was complete and Katie was at home with us in Connecticut. During this recuperation her nausea and vomiting surpassed even her most horrific times and no medications relieved her. Because Katie's immune system was completely compromised, she contracted the flu. As a last resort measure, Dr. Johnson wrote a script for twenty marijuana pills – a medication generally successful in eliminating extreme nausea in cancer patients. After ingesting one pill, Katie began hallucinating. It scared Dick; he dialed 911. I didn't want him to but he had to do what he had to do. (Periodically we struggled with our own separate opinions about Katie's treatments, and we did it with volume.) Nevertheless, shouting now and then beats moping, sighing all the time, and giving up.

The ambulance pulled in at midnight. With its red lights flashing and twirling, three EMS guys tore through our front door. I directed them to Katie in the family room. They walked up to her. Their eyes assessed her IV pole, her slim body covered in blankets, the situation. I watched them glance at one another, shake their heads compassionately. Two of the fellows seemed about Katie's age - they sat on the floor, putting them eye-level with her as she lay on the couch. The third older man stood next to Dick and me. They could see Katie was having a reaction to the drug probably because they had helped other young kids through "bad trips" but we could see they knew that this was different.

Katie remained on her side and even while sick as a dog, even while bald as a little chick, even while her big turquoise eyes were completely dilated she batted them coquettishly. But seeing Katie's fuzzy head lying child-like on the pillow, her health so fragile, and her face so sweet, made Dick and me feel completely broken. Indeed parents are only as happy as their least happy child and Dick and I were no exception. But we contained our sorrow while the EMS fellows took Katie's pulse, her blood pressure and her temperature. They stayed for about an hour until they were certain that Katie was out of the scary part of coming down off the drug. Then, one by one, they squatted down and touched her hand to say good bye after which they picked up their medical equipment and stood up to leave. Dick walked them to the door, shaking their hands with thanks.

September 15, 1999
Dear Katie,

After the EMS guys left, you slipped off to sleep but quickly bolted upright shouting, "Mom, someday YOU will be the President, but take this advice tonight, WATCH YOUR BACK UNTIL THEN‼" Then you grinned at me, you funny woman, and fell back to sleep. I smiled knowing you felt safe again. Then I glanced over at your nightstand where staring back at me was one of David Baldacci's books. Knowing his considerable use of espionage content, I suspected that the story and the hallucinations were all mixed in there together. "Will you stay next to me tonight, Mom? I don't want to see those terrible monsters again."

"Of course, Darling, not to worry, you'll be perfectly safe; I'll sleep right here, right here by your side." And so I did. And so you slept.

Love,
Mom

I always felt so close to Dick as I observed him loving Katie, loving Richard. He was never jealous of all the attention I gave to our kids right from the start. A wife can feel that; she knows the difference. As a couple we worried about Richard because his nature was sweet and sensitive and because the reality of our time with Katie naturally meant that there was less time to focus on him. We did our best staying involved with Rich's life, but Katie was diagnosed in 1989 so we're not just talking about a year or two. I think this sibling situation is more complex in terms of time and attention when the other children are younger.

Looking back, I realize how lucky I was marrying someone

like Dick. His steadfastness and dependability alone made the choice a lasting one and, unconsciously, it felt familiar to me. We always go to the familiar, unless we are living a very conscious existence, and at twenty years of age when we met I wasn't terribly conscious. Fortunately, Dick's positive traits were ones of strength and integrity - traits I consistently experienced in my own mother and Dick clearly had the best of her plus he was enormous fun like my father.

Yes, dear Reader, Dick and I have been traumatized by our daughter's illness. And like other parents who have witnessed their child go through physical and emotional turmoil this vast and prolonged and have seen the sick child's sibling suffer the worriment too, we know that we shall never be the same again. And how could we be? We know for sure that love exacts a cost.

Katie and I often discussed our lives. A cancer diagnosis alerted Katie to what might happen to her: a premature death and she didn't need reminders. Before the second stem cell transplant there was

~Looking Back Reflections ~

When I recall this time period, which was spent between Connecticut and Manhattan, I realize how different the experience could have been if I had picked a selfish husband. Honestly, I think who we choose as a mate might be the most important decision that we ever make.

concern that malignant cells had entered her spinal fluid - which would be very bad - so an X-Ray of her spine was ordered. The doctor, who had known Katie for years, insensitively commented, "Well, Katie, you'll never die of old age." He was responding to a question Katie had asked him like, "How does it look?" and he gave his nasty response. It hurt her and it made her angry, a rarely expressed emotion for Katie. He made his remark out of my earshot and I was furious when Katie told me. But she made me swear I would say nothing to him. "It's really okay, Mom, I just won't invite him to sit on my medical board once it is in place."

Then Katie and I had a discussion about people who say stupid and hurtful remarks to others, like "everything happens for a reason" or "something good always comes out of something bad" or worse, implying that someone's emotions caused the illness, whatever the malady. Our eyes always locked in those moments. I would mumble that they should see the kids missing limbs like the seven year old girl we shared Thanksgiving dinner with in the cancer ward one year. Or even spend a week at any children's hospital in palliative care and then let them tell me how emotions played into that. It makes me fighting mad.

Katie, however, would pensively shrug her shoulders, elevate her chin, and purse her lips, "Mother, they're ignorant." But her mother? Well, only angels held her mouth shut.

September 17, 1999
Dear Katie,

There were many times I didn't want you far from me because I, like most mothers, believed when my children were close by they were safe; nothing bad would happen to them. But bad things do happen in this world, even when the mom is close. [3] You asked me, more than once, Katie, "Mom, when people are suffering and needing some compassion, why do you think other people gloss over it?" After I gave you a little tweak on the nose I responded, "I suppose, darling Katie, they just haven't suffered enough yet."

Love,
Mom

No malignant cells were discovered in Katie's spinal fluid. It was now January 1997, and time for her second stem cell. Everyone dreaded poor Katie having to go through it once again. Oh, God, I just wanted to get her back to Connecticut to recuperate and have a life that looked somewhat normal for her and all of us again. I was also unsuccessful locating

---

3 *Necessary Losses, p. 22*

another apartment near the hospital on such short notice given that now her treatments were stretched out an additional month. Concerned about what to do, our hospital social worker recommended the NYC Ronald McDonald House. I thought it would sure beat a hotel for thirty days. Of course, that was before I discovered I would be sharing the kitchen with many other women, none of whom spoke English.

There is a running joke about two women being incompatible in a kitchen together. Well, we had five counting me. Like armored guards these formidable ladies stood erect with arms wrapped tightly around their large, low-slung bosoms. As they muttered under their breath and jerked their heads in my direction, I wanted to throw holy water all over myself. After a week of feeling like the devil himself, I simply stopped trying to engage them and eventually wrote off their unfriendliness to stress, both theirs and mine. Besides, it was effort enough focusing on the task at hand in this tight 8 x 10 foot kitchen where every pot, every bottle, every food item and medication had to be labeled to separate Katie's items from the other children's. Yes, my pretty kitchens over the years had definitely spoiled me, and while I tried to be a big girl most days and just suck it up, I felt like I would have killed for a chilled glass of chardonnay, a Philly hoagie, and a big bag of Herrs Potato Chips.

Sometimes I found my thoughts turning negative; when they did I quickly pulled them back and forgave myself because a crowded kitchen with a few unhappy faces seemed a lame excuse for being disagreeable. Besides, there was "something" exceedingly larger going on here other than Katie's illness and a few negative thoughts. Yes, without a doubt there was a "something," and that "something" was love.

September 20, 1999
Dear Katie,

Remember the night at the Ronald McDonald House when you laughingly told me that when you and Richard were teenagers, all your friends thought your father and I were the strictest parents that they knew? I gave you my reasons for being strict, I really did. I told you your safety came first so there would be a curfew. I told you no drinking until it was legal. I told you to never disrespect yourself for anyone no matter what. And I told you that they were reasons enough! You said, "Mom those reasons make no sense!"

But, Katie, I tried explaining to you that as most girls taught by nuns would know, I was the kind of girl

who gave up making out for Lent, that should have told
you something right there.

Love,
Mom

The second stem cell went more quickly than the first.
Once complete and Katie was strong enough to leave, we flew
out of the Ronald McDonald House like bats flying out of a Tran-
sylvania cave. Back in Connecticut, Katie began resembling her
old self again, despite the fact that she hadn't a single hair on her
head and the scars on her scalp were deep, dark pink and omi-
nous. It was during this period that Katie used her "recuperating" time to meet with some people who worked in organizations
which helped children. She wanted to gather more information
to see where a cause-related marketing program could be useful
alongside of children's needs.

One morning she asked for the car because she had
arranged a meeting at Dana-Farber Cancer Institute in Boston,
Massachusetts. I was reluctant to let her go because she was still
a little shaky. But I was aware, too, that here was that Katie Brant
who wanted to get on with her life. I handed Katie the keys,
"Please drive carefully."

Her meeting went well in Boston. It prompted another meeting in Westport, Connecticut with yet another agency - Save the Children. I felt more comfortable handing Katie the keys this time because it was only twenty minutes away. Several hours later Katie walked excitedly in the door, "Mom, I met the most incredible woman who asked me if I would be interested in working with her at UNICEF!" I didn't see the connection immediately but Katie explained that it was the director she sweet talked into giving her some time with and that this woman was seriously considering a professional career move into Manhattan. She told Katie during this "information gathering" that she could bring some people in with her whom she felt had the heart to help children. Remember that line from the movie *Jerry Maguire*, "You had me at hello"? Katie had her at hello.

Several weeks later Katie quite her job at Time Inc. and signed on. In the second breath she informed us that she had found a new apartment in Chelsea and could we help her move out of The Village and into it. "It has a Murphy Bed and a doorman!" Dick and I smiled, rolled up our sleeves and helped Katie pack and move her stuff out and down five flights of floors feeling positive all the while. It was during this same period my husband's boss took a new job in Philadelphia. I started packing the night Dick told me his boss was leaving because I felt wonderful changes were in the air. My husband thought I was a witch. "I am," I winked, "but a good witch."

Dick gave his notice at work and soon moved into a temporary living apartment in Philadelphia while we waited to move into our new home in the Philadelphia suburbs. When the trucks arrived on moving day to take us back to Philadelphia, I literally jumped up and down in the driveway like some lunatic because we were "going home." The only hard part for me moving was leaving some wonderful new friends and clients. But the timing was right because now Katie had returned to work in Manhattan and while tired, she was excited for another chance to live her big city life. Katie's youth worked for her here because even after this long ordeal, her stamina miraculously returned. And quite frankly, I am always ready to move. It's a great adventure for me. I told my brother-in-law Jim that the sound of tape being wrapped around a moving box was absolutely thrilling. He kidded me with his reply saying my moving was a sickness.

Several months after we settled back in Pennsylvania, Katie called me on her lunch hour. "Hi Mom, what do you say we go to Ireland?" It was something we had talked about during her stem cell treatments. I called a travel agent and discussed an Ireland itinerary then I called Katie back. "Guess what, Sweetheart, I found a great bus tour!" Katie's response, "Oh, forget the bus, Mom, you and I are renting a car for a drive around!" Dick smiled at our invitation to join us both but took a pass while Katie and I packed up and headed for the Emerald Island.

Our first stop was Dublin where we relaxed and watched the gentle Princess Diana's funeral on TV after which Katie took a nap and I headed out for a stroll and a haircut. The following day we took off for the pretty town of Killarney where a festive banner with "Congratulations Kate" hung across the street to greet us when we arrived. Similar signs with "Welcome Kate!" and "Kate's the One" were spread about the town in every store window. We smiled realizing that Ireland was showing us its magical side. I actually thought Dick had something to do with it but it turned out to be the announcement of a new computer system for the community, but what awesome timing!

Two days later we drove down to the charming southern coast of Ireland and stayed a couple of nights in Kinsale. There we met the owner of our first bed and breakfast. "Welcome to Seashore House, I'm Mary Hurley!" Katie and I looked at one another wide-eyed because my maiden name was Mary Hurley! As we enthusiastically told Mrs. Hurley the coincidence, Katie and I simultaneously threw our arms around this stout freckled woman as though she were kin. She was startled all right and asked us if we had had a pint at lunch! We answered, "No but we're ready for one now!"

"Well hurry up yourself then to pub at the bottom of the hill because I own it and the first one is on the house!" A few hours later we walked to the pub where freckled-face Mrs. Hurley tended the bar. Happy to see us she kept generously pouring me one too many. Sweet Jesus, Mary and Joseph, as the Irish say, within the hour I felt as if I were at another big Hurley family party! I sang too loud with the band, danced too hard by my chair and requested one too many Irish ballads. Honestly it was delightful! But dear Reader, it unnerved Katie. Sometimes it is not just parents who are disconcerted seeing their kids do or say things, sometimes it is the kids that don't like seeing their parents outside of their ordinary roles.

"Mom, you're flirting and drinking too much!" Our roles had switched - Katie was now parenting me, the bad teenager. Well, I got mad, I really did. It was the first time since Katie had relapsed years before that I had been upset with her. Ask anyone who is in a caretaking role with someone they love. It is difficult to be mad at someone who is sick so at some level, this was probably a healthy response.

Admittedly, I was defensive about her comment because, actually, I think Katie was right.

chapter **Seven**

When the storm strikes a rooster, he folds up; he just endures it,
wrapping his wings about him to protect himself as best he can,
just drooping through to the dreary end.

When the storm strikes an eagle, he has another spirit; he spreads
his wings and makes the winds carry him high above the storm.
The same choice is ours.

~J. WALLACE HAMILTON, RIDE THE WILD HORSES~

During the last of the winter of 1998 Katie's improving health evoked a singular sigh of relief throughout our entire circle of family and friends. Paralleling this period was also the uplifting news of Richard and Caroline's engagement. In this new era of hope we threw our son and future daughter-in-law an over-the-top party with a piano player, dancing and every good thing. Two months later a friend of Caroline hosted a bridal shower.

When the date for the shower arrived I picked Katie up at the train station. Sliding gingerly into the car she announced, "Mom, I ate some rotten seafood on the train; it upset my stomach." Seafood on a commuter train? Suspicious as I drove away from the curb she directed me, "Pull over, Mom, pull over; I'm feeling sick." At the shower I watched Caroline bubbling over with happiness. I also watched Katie with a keen awareness that what I had witnessed at the train station had nothing to do with shrimp, or crab or tuna fish.

September 23, 1999
Dear Katie,

I kept my concern about your becoming sick before the shower to myself. The next day you took an early train back to your job in New York City and again became sick; this time at your desk. You called Dr. Finlay and he arranged for an emergency MRI. When you called us that night your news was bad, very bad: the MRI confirmed that the tumor was back; that was why you had thrown up. We were heartsick. Had the stem cell rescue been worthwhile? You thought so; you said yes to everything if you thought it offered a cure. If it couldn't benefit you, you felt the data would help other kids. But Sweetheart, I won't start lying to you now, that call prompted a shift in my spirit - I felt your future looked bleak.

Another surgery was scheduled for you and three weeks later our family gathered again in New York for dinner before you checked in once more at New York University Hospital. It was March 1998 and three and one-half weeks away from the wedding. The 'we' was Rich, Caroline, Dick, Peter Stewart - your best male friend from Colgate - and I. We stayed positive throughout the entire evening because of your lead. Dear Chip was regrettably no longer in the picture. That was a loss and I knew you missed him as we all did. He has such enormous integrity and goodness. You said it was time for you two to separate but not because you didn't love him, because you did, as we all did and still do.

As many people know, Katie, sometimes love just isn't enough to sustain a relationship because love relationships are extremely complex. Positively speaking, six years was a wonderfully long time. To this day I truly believe that Chip was the husband of your soul.

I know it saddened you immensely, Katie, when

you and Chip were over as a couple and while you shared some of the pain with me, I never crossed a boundary to talk about your personal relationships unless you initiated the discussion because everyone has a right to privacy, especially the older we become. Besides, you always called out my name when you needed me.

This fifth surgery was a twelve-hour ordeal. I slept in the waiting room the first and second nights, nothing new there; it's what I did after every surgery. There, while The Big Apple slept, I could see you and you could see me. St. John of the Cross once said, in the evening of life we will be judged on love alone, and difficult as it was seeing you in intensive care again, my first born child whom I loved beyond my fear, beyond my sorrow, I also knew there was something in your spirit so other worldly, so without self-pity and guile that I was drawn to be there at your side. It was not a sacrifice for me, Katie, it was oxygen.

On Day Five we left NYU Hospital and brought you home to Villanova. It was three weeks before Rich and Caroline's wedding. Once more, I dressed your head wound. Once more I held a straw to your mouth. Once more we tried joking and concentrating on the wedding. Holding those separate worlds together: your recuperation and Rich and Caroline's big day, meant stepping away from a serious reality that you had just completed your fifth brain surgery - five horrible and terrifying operations. During this recovery you were listless, shaky, and constantly freezing even though we set the heat to 80 degrees. My normally wavy hair reacted immediately to the new stress: it went poker straight. One morning I said to your dad, "Katie's not bouncing back this time, Dick." Your dad looked at me, put his head down and shook it from side-to-side; I knew he saw it too.

At last the wedding day was here: April 18, 1998 - an absolutely glorious morning with billowy clouds high in an intensely blue sky. Your dad helped your brother put on his tuxedo tie, snap some pictures, then off to the church we went. I watched your brother's beautiful bride walk up the aisle. My gaze moved from her radiant face, to Rich's smiling one, to your wobbling feet. There you stood at the altar as Caroline's Maid of Honor. There you swayed - back and forth, back and forth - as the congregation held its breath. Then it was my turn. I read from The Song of Solomon, "Rise up, my love, my fair one, and come away, for lo, the winter is past." But the winter wasn't past for our family and everybody knew it.

At the reception Richard and I danced to "What a Wonderful World." Inside myself I questioned, was I being a good enough mother today? I prayed that I was. Your sensitive and handsome brother who always made me laugh, feel loved and asked for so little. Oh Lord above, why must everything be so complicated, Katie?

When the mother and son dance was over I scanned the room for you, Katie. I asked around. "Have you seen Dick? Have you seen Katie?" Then I spotted your dad outside the ladies' room. "Is something wrong, Dick?"

"Yes, Katie's in there throwing up the eight cups of coffee she drank to stay awake." I hugged your dad and we cried a little together. I asked him to see if our good friends Tammy and Robin could take you home and stay with you until Rich and Caroline left for their honeymoon. As you know, Robin was a wonderful physician and he and Tammy loved you, Sweetheart. That idea comforted your dad who smiled shyly and nodded his head. Then I gently took his hand in mine and led him back to the dance floor where we did what lovers do - dance and cling to one another.

Love,
Mom

~Looking Back Reflections ~

I learned so much during this period about the difference in being a mother to a son and a mother to a daughter. I learned to take a gracious second place in my son's life after he married realizing that Richard had embarked on his new life, he had left home and taken a wife and I wanted to give him that psychological freedom to be the man and the husband he had become. We mothers have the power to either release or hold.

With Katie as my daughter I was intuitively confident that our feminine souls would always reflect one another. There was never a need or reason for me to compete at any stage with Katie or, heaven forbid, to make her please me by being another Mary Jane. I knew who Katie was and she knew who I was. We took the time to really see one another and grow with one another.

Friendship developed with both of my grown children during this period. I learned to make the switch from mother to friend because they showed me that was what they wanted from me now. Looking back I was surprised to realize how important it was to me that they liked the woman that I was too, not just the mother. I try still to be a person that my grown children would want to have dinner with, share a conversation with, confide a vulnerability with. I suppose this time engrained in me to take nothing for granted. This mother did learn from the children.

After the wedding, Katie's recuperation continued with us in Villanova for another three weeks. It was still the spring of 1998 and everyone's lives were moving forward: the newly-weds had returned from their island honeymoon and moved to Georgetown in Washington, DC and Katie and I were headed to New York City for her post-surgical appointment with Jeff Wisoff, MD. Katie planned to make her decision about returning to work after her meeting with him. I felt so grateful sitting in this very same waiting room, children's storybook pictures all around. You see, dear Reader, nine years ago we had been informed that statistically Katie's type of anaplastic astrocytoma gave her an eighteen month survival rate.

On this day Katie looked great and felt great. With locked arms, we laughed freely and hysterically about a discussion we had had in the cab ride from the train station. When her surgeon Dr. Wisoff's receptionist Carla kept eying us curiously, we invited her into our conversation. The topic was about kissing. "Carla," Katie said, "may I ask you a technical question about kissing?" (Carla started laughing too because, trust me, not only were we contagious but everybody needs a laugh working in pediatric oncology.)

"Sure, shoot, I don't know if I'm an expert or anything" - as her smile broadened - "but I'll answer if I can." Then Katie narrowed her eyes as her face took on a serious expression,

"Carla, can you still call it 'making out' if you're not French kissing?" Katie covered my mouth now so that I would pipe down.

"Well," Carla pondered, "technically, I suppose you can." Katie blurted out, "What? What? You just rub lips together! No way!" And we laughed and nudged one another. Yes, we were all thirteen years old that day and we all needed to be thirteen years old that day. Katie and I used every excuse to clown around. Yes folks, New York City was a happening – uptown, downtown, cross-town. No negative statistic could stop this team from reaching its goal. Katie and M.J., we hung tough; it was the stuff we were made of.

But by now I'm certain you can see, dear Reader, just how often Katie's health swung from bad to good or from good to bad. These unpredictable roller coaster rides we had to accept and buckle ourselves in for because they were part of her health picture. The serenity to accept what we cannot change reality. It was shortly after the post-surgical visit that Katie again needed another emergency hospitalization because she felt weak and shaky. By then, Dr. Finlay had left Memorial Sloan Kettering to become New York University's Director of Hassenfeld Children's Center for Cancer and Blood Disorders. So where Jonathan Finlay went, Katie went, I went, and Dick went. Extensive testing indicated Katie had dangerously low sodium levels. It was Memorial Day Weekend, a warm night, and Dick and I need-

ed to de-stress after Katie feel asleep. We walked to a neighborhood martini bar and sat outside.

Sipping our cold drinks we discussed how we didn't want
to spend the next several months again living like two gypsies
in New York trying to manage Katie's treatment, traveling back
and forth, working, and living in hotels. We needed a home base.
That evening, as summer officially began, we mutually decided to have Katie treated back in Philadelphia. We knew no one
would like it. We were right. "Mr. and Mrs. B., we are against it,"
said her entire medical team. "Katie's brain had caused her to
'waste salt,' therefore we need to implement a sophisticated plan
to place her on constant IV sodium infusion."

The doctors in Manhattan loved Katie which made it more
difficult to leave. Plus Katie wanted to be treated in NYC where
her friends and co-workers lived and she made no bones about it.
We told her that when she was well she would once again return
to NYC and we would all work together to that end. When Katie
finally agreed, Doctor Sharon Gardner arranged for a medical
team to transport Katie by ambulance back to Philadelphia. Her
other doctors said they would stay involved with Katie's Philadelphia physicians and treatment. On the trip down the New
Jersey turnpike I sat up front with the driver and watched Katie
laughing and flirting outrageously with the two ambulance guys
in the back requesting them to turn the sirens on and off for her.

Dick pulled up next to us in his car smiling and waving at Katie and me.

As I watched the NYC skyline disappear behind us I blew him a kiss and inhaled a deep breath for the strength to meet whatever challenge lay before us. I closed my eyes and prayed to God to get you well, please once more, just get you well. Then I chuckled and felt strengthened remembering how Lance Armstrong had not only survived his horrendous cancer but said in his book, that there are angels on this earth, and they come in subtle forms.[4] Yes, I thought, while I listened to the boisterous laughter coming from Katie and the ambulance guys, and some angels blow trumpets and some push siren buttons in ambulances.

When the ambulance pulled into our driveway a home healthcare nurse stood ready to demonstrate Katie's new equipment. She said it should do the trick and that there would be no problems. She was wrong. Twenty-four hours later, Katie began to throw up, and then her projectile vomiting became severe enough to warrant my taking her to the emergency room of our local hospital. Dick left work to meet us there.

The admitting doctor in ER knew nothing about the complexities of a long-term brain tumor patient or Katie's situation in particular. He asked her ridiculous questions like, "Where do *you*

---

4 *It's Not About the Bike: My Journey Back to Life,* p.151).

want to live, Katie? Did you like living in New York City?" Naturally we were defensive because we felt guilty taking Katie from her beloved New York City. Katie's response to the doctor was that she *loved* her New York apartment and wanted to live *there.* Katie was an adult in her late twenties and of course she missed her independent life enormously, but she was also extremely ill and this clueless man treated her request as a distinct possibility. He said he would even make arrangements to get her back there! Dick was livid. He called Dr. Finlay and brought him up to date.

Dr. Finlay said he had an old colleague at Children's Hospital of Philadelphia, Anna Janss, M.D., PhD. He said he would call her to come visit Katie in the hospital which Dr. Janss did the next day. Katie liked her immensely and asked Anna to be her doctor and Anna, God bless her, said yes. And believe me; saying yes to treating Katie - with her accompanying file the size of a Webster's Dictionary - was no small commitment.

In the local hospital Katie's health deteriorated overnight. The local hospital did not understand her condition; we knew we had to get her out of there and into Children's Hospital of Philadelphia. Dick said, "I'm calling Children's Hospital, Mare." I nodded my head. He asked for Neuro-oncology and told them that our local hospital was not treating Katie properly and that they had refused to discharge her! When he hung up, his smile was as broad as Texas. He said the department doc at Children's

Hospital told him, "Oh, don't worry Mr. Brant; we'll get Katie out of there!" In less than an hour, Katie and I were in an ambulance en route to Children's Hospital, her original hospital of nine long years ago. Dick drove behind us always protecting Katie, always watching her back.

Dr. Janss became her official doctor of record along with Doctors Jean Blasco and Beverly Lang. Once admitted Katie's physicians in New York and Philadelphia conferenced and concurred about exactly where her sodium levels needed to remain. This was vital for controlling the fatal side effects of sodium depletion. Two weeks later Katie had improved and was discharged with a portable pump for sodium infusion. This was when Margie Rose, R.N., a senior Children's Hospital of Philadelphia nurse, entered our lives.

Margie's job was to instruct us in the use of the pump - a machine which was attached to a quart size sodium bag that Katie carried around like a large purse. The plastic tubes on the bag connected to veins deep within her chest. She called that bag her ball and chain and it was, because every day I hooked her up to it for ten to twelve hours.

In general I'm challenged by machinery and this one freaked me out completely because I didn't want my incompetence to cause something horrible to happen to Katie. Margie assured me that I would get it down, "Believe it or not, even people who aren't real smart learn how." Wah! Now that was a different kind of pressure! But Margie kept me sane with her even disposition and excellent nursing skills. "He has given His angels charge over thee...." (Psalm 90:11) Well, God did send an angel to watch over our Katie and her name was Margie Rose.

~Looking Back Reflections ~

I am astounded when I think of all the people who entered our lives, exceptional people in the medical world and maybe not of this world all together. This was the place where I drew the most confidence; when I learned to let control go and trust. I think having the right people in our lives, when we needed them, was key to my very survival.

The princess grew, and all the gifts of the fairies were fulfilled.
She became so beautiful, intelligent, and pure of heart
that everyone who saw her could not help but love her.

~SLEEPING BEAUTY –
A TREASURY OF CHILDREN'S LITERATURE~

Yes, everyone fell in love with Katie. People always wanted to be Katie's friend and they often sought her counsel. She
adored having friends come by because she could not get out of
the house very often now. When people are ill and, consequent-
ly, spend days, weeks and months in bed, their world shrinks; so
it's a lovely gesture to bring the world to them. Visiting the sick,
that sacred corporal work of mercy, may not cure a patient's malady but it surely helps alleviate some of his or her misfortune.
Katie, like most patients, looked for our smiles and good will. She
looked for special goodies, interesting stories, and outside news.
And we brought them to her because treating Katie royally was
easy - she was everybody's princess.

September 28, 1999
Dear Katie,

How you loved big breakfasts and those days you
wanted that fresh cup of joe to lift the fog of your medications. One morning you said, "Mom, I don't hear very
well and I only see out of one eye plus there are a few
other things not working real great, but if I stayed just
the way I am now I could continue to do this, could you?"
The directness of your question stunned me because I
knew you were concerned about me. Unhesitatingly I
responded, "Of course, darling Katie, of course I could

continue to do this. It never crossed my mind for a second that I could not." We hugged one another then and you know, Katie, with that statement you and I believed we would have our life together for a long, long time; that what we believed we could somehow make happen just by virtue of our saying it. And, with the power of that belief we could keep your life on hold, precious Katie, keep your life on hold.

Love,
Mom

Yes, keeping Katie's life on hold was our m.o. In addition to the sodium situation we were also deeply concerned about the tumor growing. That obviously meant that Katie needed a new chemotherapy protocol strong enough to eradicate her tumors, yet tolerable enough for her now fragile body to withstand. As we waited for one to become available, Katie lived with us. We also kept the Chelsea apartment and told Katie so she would know that we all still had the hope of her returning to New York City. But, dear Reader, Katie was much too ill for even a return visit.

Most nights Katie's delicate condition - which was becoming more evident - frightened away sleep for me. During the day we stayed busy with games, movies, conversations and hugs, lots of hugs. Then one particularly quiet afternoon, Katie walked quietly into the kitchen looking a little down - heaven knows she had every right to. She told me she felt like Sisyphus. He was the Greek god who was condemned to push an enormous bolder up a steep hill only to watch it roll down again at the end of every day.

"Katie," I said, as I looked at her, "I can understand that these relapses are absolutely a repeating torture." She shook her head and blinked back a few tears. I put down my paring knife, took her hands in mine. Looking into her beautiful face I said, "My precious Katie, let's think about a few things here. Your determination and belief in cause-related marketing helped you to negotiate a promotion and a new post and the title of 'Cause Related Marketing Specialist at TIME, Inc.'! And you were in a hospital bed when you did it! Amazing. You are amazing.

"Plus, your tireless networking and continued diligence then positioned you into your next business opportunity and introduced you to UNICEF's new Senior VP of Marketing and Development. This esteemed past director of Save the Children then personally recruited and hired you as her assistant, awarding you the deserved title, 'National Director of Corporate Marketing.' Unbelievable. And you managed these amazing accomplishments despite horrific obstacles to your health!"

Katie smiled sweetly and nodded her head up and down, which I took to mean she accepted my observations concerning her important history. But as her mother, her Sisyphean reality saddened me terribly because I knew she was wrestling with resigning this newly acquired position at UNICEF which would be yielding to the strong possibility that she felt she wasn't going to get well. That was deeply painful for me; I cannot begin to imagine what it was for dear Katie.

The pressure escalated for her. The reality of a high powered executive position, which demanded lots of energy and ideas, preoccupied her waking moments because while she had a thousand ideas, the disease had her energy. "Mom, my personal integrity will not allow me to have Diane, my new boss, hold my spot open any longer. I'm calling her today to resign." She sobbed after hanging up from the call and I suspect Diane and all of Katie's new friends there did, too. Indeed, Katie and her boss were a powerful package of great promise and each held mutual fondness and respect for the other. Such a loss for our Katie.

After a few days, a few more tears, some more hugs and Diet Cokes, Katie opened up a conversation. "Mom, do you think I might be eligible for a 501(C)(3) tax classification for a non-profit organization?" (That was the essential document for beginning a charity fund, allowing donors to treat the contribution as a charitable deduction.) "Absolutely," I told her. But in truth, I didn't have a clue what a 501(C)(3) even was.

Katie applied for the classification. Our den was then transformed into her new office and we raced against the clock knowing that those tumors had grown through every treatment and experimental therapy available. Not only that, but many of these later treatments made Katie unbelievably ill, particularly an experimental therapy which caused a fungus to develop in her lungs - the treatment for it requiring her to be on another radical IV infusion many hours every day for a month. The nurses called it "Shake and Bake" because the patient swings between chills and fever.

During this period Katie's focus remained riveted on setting up her foundation and getting that 501(C)(3) status. There was also a nerve-racking delay obtaining the 501(C)(3). When the wait became ridiculously prolonged, Dick decided to find out why. That was when he discovered that the highly recommended attorney that Katie had retained had set her legal paperwork aside. It caused enormous distress for Katie because this was precious time that she just did not have to waste. Katie's upset devastated her father. He immediately elicited Pennsylvania Congressman Curt Weldon's help. Katie, holding unsteadily onto her father's arm in Congressman Weldon's office, passionately announced that she wanted the 501(C)(3) and the fund's name to be "Katie's Kids!" When a quick search discovered the name was already taken, they left too disappointed to talk about another name. But later that day her brother said, "What about adding 'for the Cure' as a differentiation?"

Katie's Kids for the Cure became official right before Christmas 1998, in time for year end donations with a tax benefit. Soon thereafter Katie organized her impressive medical and advisory board, accomplishing this quickly and efficiently because she had set it up that way from the beginning with her dynamic personality and tremendous vision. Several private foundations and numerous friends backed her financially. Channel 6/Action News of Philadelphia picked up her story for TV and the Philadelphia Inquirer; the Suburban and Wayne Times and Main Line Life did interviews for their respective papers. Shortly thereafter Katie was nominated for a highly prestigious award for a graduate from a Catholic school education in the Archdiocese of Philadelphia. She was chosen and won, the youngest recipient ever, over numerous high profile individuals three and four times her age.

Naturally all this publicity worked well for Katie's foundation which she formed specifically to find a cure for brain tumors in children. The donations collected by Katie's Kids for the Cure are used to fund innovative and creative brain tumor research, both clinical and basic science. There are only three other research funds at all similar in the United States. Her medical board, who determines the recipients of these research grants, is comprised of several of the leading doctors and pediatric institutions in the world. Katie's entire board respected and valued her determination and commitment to this non-profit endeavor while she personally struggled to get well.

Donations by the hundreds poured in daily. She read every letter out loud to me. "Maybe someday there will even be an endowment, Mom!" I told her that no doubt that would someday be true. She smiled and gave me a little kiss and her famous wink before putting her head down for a long nap in the warm afternoon sun. I sat at the end of the couch and read; keeping one hand on her socked feet so she knew that I was there, always knew that I was there. Katie's foundation was her passion and her destiny. Like Joan of Arc once said, "I am not afraid...I was born to do this." Doesn't that have a Katie Brant undertone, dear Reader.

By late December 1998, Katie and Katie's Kids for the Cure had inspired $80,000 in contributions. Now it was time to talk to the President of her medical board, Dr. Jonathan Finlay, about awarding the first grant.

October 1, 1999
Dear Katie,

Those tireless hours researching cause-related marketing in the New York Public Library were paying off for you and while I knew squat about the nonprofit sector, I knew how to encourage your dreams. So while you focused your energies on the fund, our family waited for an available and efficacious new treatment.

One morning, as I removed you from your sodium bag and flushed your ports, you quietly said to me, "Mom, I do miss New York City but I love being here with you." What a beautiful thing to say to me, Katie. I told you then how I adored having you with me, how I loved you so very much and how you made every day perfect, absolutely perfect. That conversation was a defining one for me, Sweetheart. It was the moment I realized you had surrendered completely to your life circumstances.

I have always believed in you and your ideas, Katie. That won't stop now because I can't see you, because I know you can see me. Your foundation will succeed, darling Katie. It will succeed and it shall provide the creative research that discovers a cure for pediatric brain tumors, your mission statement. You asked me twice, "Mom, can you help me to get there?"

"Yes, Katie," I responded, and I continue to say, "Yes, yes, yes."

Love,
Mom

Katie and I had sweet little rituals for making our moments together special. One ritual offered us frequent comfort. It focused around the roses in our garden during her two summers with us. Many mornings I had a glorious task: find Katie a pretty rose. Scissors in hand, I snipped a red Lincoln or an ivory Peace Rose and onto Katie's breakfast tray they went. I would walk happily into her room. The sight of a scrumptious breakfast with its tantalizing aromas wafting off her tray along with a colorful rose caught my daughter's attention even quicker than the wolf whistles she used to get in New York City. Well, almost quicker.

October 2, 1999
Dear Katie,

Our beautiful friend, Sarah Ban Breathnatch, says that the Simple Abundance path gives us a payoff, "...we start to seek peace and comfort in the joyful simplicities. Little things begin to mean a lot to us." How fitting were her words for us for each morning as I placed the breakfast tray over your lap and gave your cheek a little kiss. "For you, little Ms. Katie, a rose for my perfect rose."

Love,
Mom

While Katie recuperated, she continued to plug her foundation. Among her biggest supporters were our good friends Ray and MarySue Hansell.

October 7, 1999
Dear Katie,

Whenever the Hansells stopped by, I'll admit that I became concerned that you would hit them up for a big check because they always asked you about your foundation. Well, you never had to ask because they got their pens out anyway. You loved playing around with Ray, Katie. I remember a funny night when you told Ray how nice he looked; that all he needed was a Bugs Bunny tie to complete his outfit. So the next day you bought him his very own Loony Tunes tie. I have to give it to you, Sweetheart; it goes really great with his new Armani suit.

Love,
Mom

Laughter kept us off the anxiety train. This is where Dick's sister Trisha came in. During Katie's two springs and summers with us, Trisha, who was plowing through a divorce, frequently stayed overnight and made herself more available to us than any other person. Our compatibility with Trisha was so agreeable that she, Dick and I bought a boat, a huge used 38 foot Carver. It had two small cabins, two baths, a little sitting room and a galley. We bought it because we wanted to have somewhere we could take Katie without restrictions and reservations. And while some people in my husband's family called our condo on the water "conspicuous opulence," we called her "The Voyager" because she allowed for a change of pace and scenery for Katie, her brother, sister-in-law, her dad, aunt and me on short notice, something we hadn't been able to accomplish in years due to Katie's sudden and frequent hospitalizations.

Katie loved the boat and always wore her "Lucky" hat, sipped Diet Cokes, ate chip and dip, and tried to catch the big one that got away.

October 10, 1999
Dear Katie,

Your Aunt Trisha is sweet, smart and positive. Your dad, Trisha and I are good friends. You and she loved talking about business - hers, yours, and the single life. Remember the night the two of you climbed into our guest bed and talked for a couple of hours? I wanted to come in that night but I didn't interfere then and I didn't interfere in your childhood friendships either. The love that you gave away and received from others in the world never belonged only to me.

Love,
Mom

chapter *Eight*

Women are always being tested...
but ultimately, each of us has to define who we are individually,
and then do the very best we can, to grow into it.

~MADELINE ALBRIGHT~

Brain tumors, brain trauma and neurological conditions are a tribulation for the patient but they carry their own set of anxieties for the caregivers. Additionally, when an illness turns chronic, daily routines need to be forced into normalcy and non-chalance surrounding them for everyone's survival. No patient needs a long suffering, martyr face around them; they feel bad enough already for changing your life and they don't need any added guilt. Therefore, complex support tasks like giving medicines, operating machines and infusions become routine and they need to be treated like a routine. It's true that the caretaker's personal life generally becomes a distant memory and these individuals often forget what their former normal life really was. But, maybe that's a good thing.

October 14, 1999
Dear Katie,

Visible changes were occurring with you, like your trance-like walking which was slower, rigid and unsteady. Tennyson's words flooded me in my distress every time I saw you get up from a chair. "O Sorrow, wilt thou rule my blood." I called Dr. Janss who told me the cause of these changes was your brain tumor. All these signs where indicators that something bad was happening, signs of your ambiguous losses, signs that little by little I was losing you. Then you began applying your lipstick differently.

One night I mentioned, nonchalantly, that you had gone a little outside of your lip line (way outside). When I picked up a tissue to fix the smudging, you looked puzzled - as though I were criticizing you. I was terribly upset because you couldn't comprehend what my attempt to help was about; you didn't see what you had done, so you thought I was acting as though you didn't know how to put on your makeup. My explaining why I did what I did would have made you more upset, so I just had to let it go, just had to keep on apologizing for being controlling, and just had to continue feeling like an evil mother.

At dinner that night you ignored me for the first fifteen minutes. That was very unlike you and it killed me. For so long I have ruminated over that event. I swear, Katie, after that night if you had worn a fish on your head I would have kept my mouth shut and worn one, too. When I'm rational enough to move away from my vain regret, I realize how few hurts or misunderstandings ever occurred between us, dear Katie, and for that I am deeply grateful. Nevertheless, I would rather die myself than ever feel that cut off from you again. Frankly, Katie, it was worse than an amputation without anesthesia.

Love,
Mom

Katie's courage to live her life to the fullest; treat it with respect, reverence and attention was inspiring and motivating. I vow to do no less. I do it for her; I do it for me.

October 20, 1999
Dear Katie,

You had Winston Churchill's courage, darling daughter, "Conquer we must - conquer we shall!" During one interview with Churchill, someone asked him what his aim was been during the war. He answered, "Victory. It is victory. Victory at all costs. Victory in spite of all terror. Victory however long and hard the road may be." [5]

One particular day an overwhelming feeling of sadness hit me fast and unexpectedly. You were unbearably sick and exhausted that morning, Katie. I knew I couldn't make you feel better, knew I couldn't change the life that you had in front of you. Oh, how many other parents suffer this also in a thousand ways with their kids! Yes, Sweetheart, on this day I found myself focused on all of your losses and simply couldn't hide my feelings. "What's wrong, Mom?" you asked,

---

5 US News & World Report, May 29, 2000

watching my averted eyes as I fluffed your pillow. "Your losses, darling Katie, all the losses you've had to suffer." A short silence ensued. You reached for my hands, looked seriously into my eyes. From your pillow, my fingers entwined in yours, you responded,

"Mom, I'd rather you focus on my victories instead."

Love,
Mom

"Katie was protected by angels," Dick said, "How else can we explain all these connections?" Well, there is a psalm, "For He ordered His angels to protect you wherever you go." (Psalms 91:11) I think that explains the day this spring when I drove five minutes away to the hairdresser while Katie talked to a friend on the phone. She was safe in her bed and having a terrific morn-

~Looking Back
Reflections ~

This encounter with Katie is forever burned into my soul because it was what she was really all about: courage. I pull this memory forward whenever I doubt or loose heart or feel my faith shake.

ing when I left or I would not have left. Then, all the way from London, a phone call came into the salon for me; it was Dick,

"Mare, don't get too upset, but an ambulance has just taken Katie to our local hospital."

How could he possibly know that from London? Well, Dick found out because Katie had called Children's Hospital Homecare and mentioned something about blood on her shirt. Alarmed because Homecare couldn't reach me, they contacted Dick's secretary who immediately called him in London and he knew where I was. Frantically, I drove to the hospital with a wet head, smeared mascara, and my leg still in a cast from a broken ankle. In seven minutes flat I arrived and pushed through the revolving ER doors. "Where is Catherine Brant please? I'm her mother."

"Catherine is in the first bed, Mrs. Brant." Immediately an unexpected composure enveloped me as I quietly pulled back the curtain. There in the bed was our Katie. "Hi Mom!" she called out, with her hands folded calmly across her abdomen, smiling, and as collected as could be. "Did you get your hair done?"

"No Darling," I responded, leaning down and giving her a little hello kiss, "I need to make another appointment; something much more important came up."

October 25, 1999
Dear Katie,

I was beyond happy seeing you behind the curtain, still grinning and as sweet as sugar cane. When the doctor walked in he smiled at you, "Katie, your IV lines have dislodged from your chest. Seems the heavy sodium in your bag snapped them clean off. It looks like you'll need to head right over to Children's Hospital and have another Broviac implant surgery.

"Oh, that's okay," you responded sweetly. It made me want to burst out in tears thinking how you always accepted these situations with such amazing grace.

I smiled down at you then as we quickly reached for one another's hands. With angelic tranquility, poise and presence, you smiled back up at me, winked, and asked for a nice icy cold Diet Coke. Suddenly the phone rang by Katie's bed; it was your father. "Is Katie okay?" he asked.

"She's okay now, Dick," I responded, "I'm in charge."

Love,
Mom

~Looking Back
Reflections ~

As I look back in time I realize how not only have I always believed in angels, but my life has demonstrated concretely how certain people are indeed angelic. When I get to the other side I suspect that there will be more angels than ordinary people who were in my life.

Dick and I marveled that so many people came together that day. Coincidences? No way. Miraculous? We thought so. We knew that there were always many angels which surrounded Katie. Did other people see this reality about her? I'm not certain but her dad and I sure did.

October 31, 1999
Dear Katie,

St. Ignatius once said, "Give me only your love and your grace; with these I will be rich enough and will desire nothing more." You exemplified that, dear Heart; you absolutely modeled that for us. In your situation you shouldn't have had a peaceful moment; yet you seemed never without peace. I feel so blessed having shared in it, been a witness to it, and your mother in it.

Love,
Mom

My childhood programmed me for vigilance; Katie's illness moved me to hypervigilance. Dick remained calm regardless. We monitored Katie's IV lines for air bubbles. I ordered and dispensed her medication. Zofran, prescribed for nausea, was the most important. It needed dispensing every eight hours exactly. In addition to sodium infusion and pills, Katie needed ongoing appointments for blood transfusions and platelets at the hospital, regular injections for increasing her red and white blood counts, and weekly clinic time at Children's Hospital for wellness monitoring. Her frequent MRIs took place late at night because Katie volunteered for inconvenient scheduling so that other kids could have the more convenient times. Dick always drove Katie and, when necessary, he donated his platelets for her.

Yes, our daughter's routines were nonstop and daunting but a mistake in any one treatment could affect her adversely for days. I became germ phobic. Like the Soup Nazi from Seinfeld, I interrogated, "Do you have a sniffle? Yes? No visit for you!" Sleep became a fantasy: anxiety and restlessness moved into my bed and my head instead - small costs for the privilege of being Katie's caretaker. Honestly, I don't mean to sound off-putting, but I must tell you, dear Reader, that taking care of Katie was like taking care of Jesus.

As the clock ticked on, Katie and I made the most of every

moment. We never missed an opportunity to say "I love you." I remember the morning Katie said, "Mom, you really are just a kid." That day she was too exhausted to lift her head from the pillow, so I put my head down next to hers. "Boy, I'm lucky," Katie said right before falling back to sleep, "How many people get to snuggle with their own private nurse."

November 5, 1999
Dear Katie,

Most days your fatigue was incapacitating. Those days I helped you to eat then I went about my normal homemaker chores: wash, clean, make a meal. Here and there I left to see a client or two. And I would worry. And I would pray. The Serenity Prayer was my most frequent resource for strength: God grant me the serenity to accept the things I cannot change. The courage to change the things I can and the wisdom to know the difference. I would converse with myself, "Can I help you make it, Katie? Will you make it; will you beat back these tumors?" Then I might hear you upstairs laughing on the phone and I'd think, "Of course you'll make it; of course you'll beat back those tumors."

During your second summer with us you slowed

down dramatically. You also appeared much younger than your twenty-eight years. Your hair was barely an inch long then and your flawless complexion gave you a luminous, celestial appearance. I remember wondering if you weren't an angel all along and not just protected by them. I mention that specifically because of the day you and I talked about heaven, the meaning of life; the meaning of death. After you shared your feelings of an intelligent God and you heard mine, you smiled and leaned in close as you took my hands in yours. Like a seer offering a prophecy, you whispered, "You still don't understand, Mom, but you will."

Love,
Mom

Behold: I feel that I have left me far behind
and shed my old life, leaf by leaf, till finally there is nothing
but the star of your smile shining richly on our life.

~RAINER MARIA RILKE, "OBLATION"~

Katie's smile changed me forever because there was an ancient story behind it. Whoever I felt I was at the start of her illness was now gone. A new more patient and more tolerant me was here now. This me only needed Katie's smile. This me only lived hour by hour now.

One morning Katie suffered a stroke. She collapsed in the shower. The stroke left bruises on her upper body and a paralysis on her left side. It left her slim arm hanging quietly by her side and her pretty upper lip drooping on the same side too. It gave Katie's sweet face a quizzical expression. She never mentioned the arm or the lip, so of course, we didn't either. This happened right before Memorial Day, 1999.

Helping her dress one day, Caroline, her sister-in-law, asked Katie if it were difficult putting that left arm through her sleeve. "Yes, Caroline, it doesn't seem to work as well as it used to."

Caroline asked me had I noticed.

"Yes, Caroline, I had, and Katie is not swallowing down all of her food anymore either."

November 6, 1999
Dear Katie,

Things were worsening. We called everybody. Days later the house exploded with friends and family kissing you goodbye. You were in your wheelchair and needed morphine that day. For some people it was the last time that they ever saw you. My friend Kathy Kirk couldn't stop crying and I loved her for it. But in true Katie form you rallied a few days later so your best friends and I threw you a women's luncheon.

Sarah Ban Breathnach came. She told you her newest book, *Something More*, was being dedicated to you and Larry Kirshbaum. She said you were the living embodiment of its glorious title. She gave you a magic wand that day. It's mine now to remember how happy you felt that day and how happy it made me when Sarah stayed the night. That evening Sarah and I became forever friends. We understood that we had a common goal and calling: love.

The following day your girlfriends Maddy, Anne, and Amy V. came and camped out in your bedroom surrounding you with rowdy stories, laughter and love. Karla, your friend from our old neighborhood, grammar school and high school, helped me for several days. New York friends stopped by: Lisa and Sam, Diane and Ginny, Deanna and Tim, E.B., her husband, Kathleen, and Peter came as well. Sometimes you were asleep; sometimes you were awake.

And while you were fragile, you were joyful and

funny every day that week repeating often how wonderful it was that so many people came to visit and how
great it was that I would throw you a party "for no reason
at all!" That was the only good thing about your brain
tumors; they seemed to remove the worst realities from
your consciousness.

Love,
Mom

My closest cousins, who are really brothers to me, Tom and
John Hurley and their wives Sandy and Irene, have made my life
so much sweeter. A few days after the luncheon, John and Irene
stopped by. "Hey, Katie," John said, "let's head into Wayne for
some of that water ice you like so much."

November 7, 1999
Dear Katie,

You felt better this day. I was so happy you went
with John. I'll never forget his rendition of your trip
into Wayne. Before pulling out of our driveway he had
asked you, "You know how to get to Wayne from here,
right Katie?"

"Sure," you responded confidently.

Two hours later, you found the water ice place that was ten minutes from our home. When you both returned, John walked through the door laughing and shaking his head about how unbelievably witty you were.

Yes, Katie you were. That wit you inherited from your father. The direction thing? Well, you inherited that gift from your mother.

Love,
Mom

Katie's ability to sustain ongoing stress was unmatched in my own personal experience. And she loved fun. The beach was a place where she always had fun. On July 1, 1999, Katie asked me to drive her down to the New Jersey shore to visit her grandparents. She spoke of many happy childhood memories in that pleasant condo on the inlet, and I was determined to get her there again. In my spirit self, I knew Katie was saying goodbye to her girlhood, her grandparents and the seashore, but we didn't talk about it. Some things are better left unsaid.

November 8, 1999

Dear Katie,

Up I pushed you into the SUV, and then we were off to Anglesea at the Jersey Shore, Katie B and her mother. What a day it was! The sun shimmered spectacularly on the incoming tide as we drove over the causeway. You said to me, "Mom, before we go to Popeye and Grandmom's, could we drive to the beach and I can look at the ocean?"

So I drove you to the spot where the inlet joins the sea. At the bulkhead I gingerly helped you from the car. You leaned on my arm, inhaled a deep breath of noon salty air and smiled. "Isn't the ocean beautiful, Mom?"

"Yes, dear Heart, it is quite beautiful," I responded.

That night we went out to dinner. You looked adorable in that little sundress with sunflowers splashed all over it. As we all chatted casually you abruptly announced, "My mom dropped me on the side of the road today!" Then you laughed and squeezed my hand. I knew you were teasing me affectionately as the waitress took our drink orders. You said, "I'll have a wine cooler, please." Your grandfather and I ordered a white wine. You took a sip of your cooler, "I don't like mine," you remarked, grabbing my wine and gulping it down.

Your grandfather smiled and put his hands tightly around his own drink announcing, "Well, a person had better hold onto their drink at this table!"

Back at the condo, your grandfather noticed you struggling to untie your sneakers. He bent over and helped you. "Popeye," you said, "I'm like an old person now, just like you." Then with the sweetest voice you added, "I couldn't walk on the beach today because the sand was too soft, but I really liked seeing it!" I just kept swallowing hard, blinking fast and trying not to cry, Katie.

At bedtime I unhooked your IV and we climbed into our twin beds separated only by a dresser. Twenty minutes later, I heard you calling out in the dark, "Mom! Mom!" I threw off my covers and leapt out of my bed but I couldn't see you; couldn't find you!

"Katie, where are you?" Then I saw you Sweetheart, on the floor wedged in between the dresser and the bed. "Darling, what‑are‑you‑doing‑on‑the‑floor?" I tried to sound calm so you wouldn't be frightened.

"I fell out of bed, Mom."

"Whoa, we'll get you right back in!"

That was your second fall in one day and a fear shot through me, but on its heels a prayer for additional muscle calmed me; I unwedged you, lifted you up and put you back into bed. Another little goodnight kiss and you were fast asleep. It was then that I saw your grandmother's silhouette in the doorway. "Is everything all right, Mom?" I asked.

"Yes, Mary," she responded as she sat down at the edge of my bed. She told me then, in a voice barely audible, that just because a family doesn't demonstrate their affection, doesn't mean that they don't feel it. Honestly, I think that was the nicest thing she ever said to me, Katie. I patted her hand and smiled.

Just then the moonlight streamed through the window as I felt the hurts of many years melt away a little bit more. That was when I think your Grandmother saw my heart in the dark, and I, gratefully, saw hers too.

Love,
Mom

As I mentioned before, dear Reader, Katie had a hundred ups and downs over the last six years. Feeling good, feeling bad. Looking strong, looking frail. Suddenly I realized how worn out I was; I realized that I needed more help, so we engaged a private nurse named Cynthia. On Day One I ran errands. In my absence Katie charmed Cynthia into ordering in every kind of junk food imaginable: hoagies, cheeseburgers, salsa and dip, fries, sodas, pizza. When I returned there was enough unhealthy greasy food for half a dozen people; I went berserk; threw some of it in the trash and asked both of them why they would buy such bad food! Katie shrugged her shoulders,

"Oh Mom, we always order out in New...York...City." Of course, she said that after she had mumbled, "Uh, oh, Cynthia, I think we're in trouble now."

Looking back I wish I had just wrapped up that stupid food and said "let's keep this half for another day." I realize now how terribly frightened I was that day because Katie's judgment was changing and I saw it. That same week Dr. Anna Janss transferred Katie into the care of Dr. Bruce Himelstein. He was designing a palliative program during this period. And while we all liked him immensely, it was Anna we were more connected to. At the time she was close to delivering her third child and it saddened her terribly seeing Katie losing ground at the same time.

The following week Bruce came by after dinner to speak with Katie and to all of us. The gloom that rainy night was oppressive as Bruce communicated to Katie that her illness had progressed - a pronouncement which surprised her because after he left she remarked, "Geez, I guess I'm a lot sicker than I thought." During and even after the meeting, Katie remained completely composed but quiet, which again, was right in character: she always took bad news calmly and courageously. The rest of us were not tranquil - we were sad and frightened. We also appreciated that the meeting was difficult for Bruce: doctors grieve when their patients don't get well. Yet that didn't stop him from telling Katie it was in her best interest to construct a living will, urging her to do it sooner rather than later.

Katie was eighteen when diagnosed with cancer, by legal definition an adult. Yet, her brain tumor had the composition and classification of a pediatric cancer. Health-wise that was the better news because overall, children's cancers have more favorable outcomes for cures and remissions. The legal part was tricky and complicated, however, because we had to handle every discussion and decision with extreme delicacy and diplomacy. Discussions with her doctors had to stay within that confidential and legal framework. This necessitated everyone walking a razor thin edge, keeping the doctors within patient confidentiality limits that their profession required, while keeping Dick and me in the driver's seat where we needed to be because eighteen was too young for monumental decision-making and Katie was too ill at twenty-eight for decision making.

The next day we made an appointment with a Philadelphia attorney to execute a living will – the document which would guide our decisions for Katie's treatment and care during her final days. Driving to the lawyer's office where Dick would meet us, Katie discussed back and forth with me what she wanted to have done: blood/no blood, resuscitation/no resuscitation. It was the most afflictive experience I have ever had in my life and it was with someone I so dearly loved.

Katie would have done anything to get well; the quality of her life seemed less important to her because she just wanted to stay alive and be with the people she loved. Dick and I appreciated the seriousness of this document that was legal and binding and we had to be clear with Katie about its contents. This discussion, even with Dick, was an agony for me; I can not begin to share with you, dear Reader, the depths to which it took me. I was sad for Katie, for Dick, for our son Richard and our daughter-in-law, Caroline. I was also sad for me; nevertheless, I would not allow sorrow to stop me from writing down Katie's wishes which we might potentially be responsible for carrying out soon.

Dick's and my love for Katie encompassed conscious awareness of her personal dignity. Who Katie was before her brain tumor was as important to us as who she was now, and no cut-and-dry document was going to usurp that. Helping Katie comprehend the grave seriousness of this discussion without inflicting a wound, a fear, or a panic necessitated the utmost sensitivity, the utmost clarity and the utmost wisdom. Katie gave Dick her first power of attorney and me the second. "Use no extraordinary means to keep me alive" was her bottom discerned line.

The days collapsed together; we lost track of time and never knew what to expect. Living in the gray world of ambiguity is difficult naturally; but when someone you love this deeply might die any day, it is torturous suffering. Some days my stress levels were so dominant I would strip down and climb into the shower just to feel the combination of hot water and steam washing over my skin. There I could have a moment of privacy and cry by myself - a practice learned long ago in my adolescence.

Then came the day when we knew our Katie couldn't be left alone, not in the evening; not in the daytime. Dick and I split the night, sleeping on a deck chaise lounge next to her bed. Rich, Caroline, family and friends came once more to be with Katie as her status went up and down, up and down.

One afternoon, Katie couldn't walk, talk or move. I was by myself with her and hysterical. I called Pat Dantz, a Children's Hospital nurse who fortunately lived nearby. We had become good friends. "Oh, God, Pat, I know it's your day off, but please come over, Katie can't move!" which she immediately did and had Katie awake, talking, and on her feet. Once more I realized the strength I drew from Katie's nurses.

The following day, Doctor Finlay called from New York. I told him of Katie's poor status. "How about I hold the phone up to Katie's good ear, Jonathan?" I discreetly turned my head away, hummed out loud and gave Katie the privacy that she deserved; that Jonathan deserved. It was the only way to proceed given that

Katie couldn't hold the phone by herself.

On July 8th, Thursday morning of that same week, Katie woke with a headache, a bad headache. She looked at me with a frightened expression, one I had never seen before. "Do you have a headache, Katie?"

"Yes, Mom, I do."

"Where is it on the pain scale, Sweetheart?"

"It's an eight, Mom." A pain scale from one to ten was our continuous guide for assessing Katie's comfort level and a course of action. I ran down the hall and got the morphine, something Katie hadn't needed for weeks. That morphine relieved her; that morphine relieved me.

November 9, 1999
Dear Katie,

I knew you trusted me completely, Sweetheart; and I didn't want you to worry, never, ever, wanted you to worry. That day and every day I kept on top of what I thought you needed but one thing I knew for certain that you never needed and that was grace, because you, dear Katie, were always in the state of grace.

God surrounded you with it your entire life.

Love,
Mom

chapter *Nine*

There is an appointed time for everything,
and time for every purpose under the heavens.
A time to be born, and a time to die; a time to plant,
and a time to uproot the plant...a time to heal...
A time to weep, and a time to laugh;
a time to mourn, and a time to dance.

~ECCLESIASTES 3:1-4~

No mother or father should have to bear the agony we bore on July 9, 1999. Katie had stopped speaking and only occasionally opened her eyes. It was clear that her prepared and perfect soul was taking its leave. Dick sat protectively and sweetly next to her bed where she could see him and he could see her. He gently held her delicate hand in his. When I entered the room to check on them, she opened her eyes. Dick, the ever present father, patted her hand and placed it down on the sheet as I moved in close.

I gently embraced dear Katie. While I held her, she picked up her two arms and placed them around me. Dick put his head into his hands and quietly wept, "Mare, Katie's bad arm is working for you." I started crying then with the awareness that the stroke which had seven weeks earlier left her arm paralyzed, she now placed completely around me. *This was a miracle and I knew it.*

Looking into my precious Katie's beautiful turquoise eyes, I told her again and again how much I loved and cherished her. She didn't respond verbally, but leaned in and gave me a sweet little kiss back. That same day, my ever-present friend Lennie arrived along with Jean Belasco, M.D. and Pat Danz, RN.

November 15, 1999
Dear Katie,

I heard Lennie ask Jean and Pat, "Is Katie in any pain?"

I heard them answer, "Katie is not suffering from any pain."

But we were, Katie, all of us in your room were in

enormous pain, especially your mother, your father, your brother and your sister-in-law.

Love,
Mom

November 18, 1999
Dear Katie,

It was July 10, 1999. As we listened to your rhythmic breathing, gazed into your face, so serene, so sweet, so precious, I thought about the blessing of having had you at home for the past two summers. I thanked God that you had received the Sacrament of the Sick not once, but twice. Yet my prayer was barely off my lips when I felt an indescribable sword pass through me. Dear sweet Jesus, how long would it be? What will we do without you, Katie? What will I do without you? That was when I heard a sound - footsteps - and they were coming up the stairs.

Running to see who it was, I gasped when I saw Margie Rose, your loyal nurse, who wasn't even scheduled for two more days. I turned and whispered sadly to your dad, "This is the day Katie will die, Dick."

"No!" he shouted. But I knew it was true and that

the Holy Spirit was preparing us both for the inevitable. Margie knew it, too; I saw it in her face and it helped me yield to the deeper meaning of her unexpected arrival: God had sent her to minister to you and to us. Margie's coming was a holy presence and *the second miracle.*

Shortly after Margie's arrival, Chrissy, Sister Nancy, Cynthia, Rich, Caroline, Dick and I formed a circle of love and prayer around your bed where for the next five hours we listened to your breathing which was labored, slow and unforgettable. There was no denying that the day I had dreaded and feared for ten years was now upon us. We patted you, we stroked your hair, and we lightly kissed your face. We took turns holding your hands. We expressed our deepest feelings to you. No one left your side. Everyone's sorrow was unbearable, but each of us contained it, for no one placed his or her sorrow above your peace.

I gazed once more upon your delicate face that I've loved for so many years. For some still unknown reason, I pulled back the covers and looked at your feet. Back a little more, I looked at your legs. Back a little more, I looked at your beautiful hands. I looked at your sacred body becoming whiter and whiter before my eyes, Katie. Your face became translucent, radiant and shone like the sun. "Can you see Katie changing?" I said, and I started crying, *"Oh my God, Katie looks like Jesus."*

Just then your breathing became even slower and slower, then...no more. Margie listened for your heartbeat, looked up at us and said, "Katie has gone."

Love,
Mom

A funeral for a loved one is a necessity. The family is in shock, even when the death is expected. The family doesn't have time for grieving; there is too much work to do: the viewing, the liturgy and the burial. There are flowers, the reception afterwards and a hundred phone calls to make. It's telling the story over and over again: the story no one wants to remember, but no one can forget.

November 19, 1999
Dear Katie,

I don't speak about that third and most important miracle I witnessed on the day you died: the transformation of your body; your face taking on the countenance of Jesus. Why is that, Sweetheart? It is just too painful to verbalize. Sometimes I think that sacred vision will have to carry me through the rest of my earthly life. Besides, it may have been revealed only to me, loving gifts from God and from you.

The day of your funeral arrived. I remember smoothing the pall over your casket as I would have smoothed your hair. I remember sliding into the pew; I remember focusing my eyes straight ahead because there was no reason to remember a scene I had envisioned a thousand times before in my mind. I remember kneeling, praying and thinking how your death had so eclipsed my father's death, my mother's death: it was so much worse. I remember hearing Caroline's praising voice and Frank Kirk's sorrowful one drifting down from the altar in their eulogies. I remember the hymn, "Jesus remember me when I come into your kingdom" and I remember crawling through every torturous moment.

Because you had requested a closed coffin, followed by a cremation and private burial of your ashes, we were forced to wait until the end of the week for our family closure. Often I've thought how those present at your funeral Mass might have preferred seeing you one last time. We couldn't do that, though, and not because of how you looked - you looked beautiful - but because you asked us not to. We honored your every wish, Sweetheart.

We catered a lunch after Mass at the Willows, a historic mansion high on a hill, a place where you and your friends hung out during your high school years. I tried being gracious to everyone that day and I think I was, but my heart and soul were really with you, Katie, only with you.

The time to bury your ashes had arrived. Standing at your grave I read aloud "Do Not Go Gentle Into that Good Night" by Dylan Thomas.

"Do not go gentle into that good night.
Old age should burn and rave at close of day;
rage, rage against the dying of the light.

As I read the verses, my voice reflected the love I had felt for you, my darling Katie, your entire life. It also reflected the passion, the anger, and the bewilderment that now engulfed me in your absence. The end of an era was at hand that day because I knew my primary job of raising you and your brother was done, was complete: Richard was married and you were with God.

Yes, Katie, your death defined the end of what I considered my greatest vocation and life's calling - being a mother. Standing there I felt completely exhausted and traumatized and a great defeat enveloped me. Yet, in another part of my spirit I felt indescribably proud of you, Sweetheart, because your life was a masterpiece in so many important ways.

But sad and proud are separate places in your mother's heart; one doesn't replace the other.

Love,
Mom

~Looking Back Reflections ~

I could barely move during this period. It was all I could do just to breathe. I felt like The Handless Maiden from the Brothers Grimm tale. The woman who walked around with matted hair, no hands, ravaged and lost. How I got through the day was by getting out of bed and burying myself in a task. I do not even remember if I spoke on the phone. I think that I did not.

The day following Katie's funeral, I wrote the first 50 of 215 thank you notes. Then I sorted through her closets. The separating, the seeing, it was a bruising task. Most items went directly to charity, specifically the St. Vincent de Paul Society. Love letters from boyfriends I burned without opening. I've heard that some people keep everything, especially if a child died, and they make a shrine out of the room. Oh, dear Reader, that is not a good idea.

One blue knit dress I decided to keep. I wrapped it in tissue paper but not before I buried my face in it and remembered Katie wearing it to my birthday party this past February. I closed my eyes and remembered how it felt to fast dance and hug her that night and every night and how she always smelled - like baby powder. Some days I miss her so much that I just shout out her name over and over again and I think I can't bear it, but bear it I must for I have no choice, dear sweet Jesus, I have no choice.

November 20, 1999
Dear Katie,

I kissed good-bye each item that you owned before I gave them away. Many of your glorious scarves went to your friend Beth but I kept a few, just in case I needed one for someone. I smile now remembering how just two months ago your dad and I took you and Beth to that Mexican restaurant on Cinco de Mayo and you ordered a margarita - short glass, mountains of salt on the lip please. The following morning you told me that after I went to bed you rung Beth up. "You did, Sweetheart?" Yes, you said, because you wanted to tell Beth you had just phoned the convent and asked the shocked sister who answered if one had to be a virgin to become a nun. Beth told me later how she chuckled and asked you why you did that. "Well Beth," you responded, "because I'm thinking about becoming a nun."

The following afternoon I called Sister Regina, a little embarrassed I must admit, Katie, but not about your question or your response, only about the late hour when you called the convent. Sister told me that the oldest nun in the house heard the phone ringing and ringing at some ungodly hour and hustled to answer it. "Well, Mary Jane," Sister Regina said, "our aging sister told your Katie that she wasn't to worry about being a virgin because that

~Looking Back Reflections ~

I think I could have slowed down about going through Katie's personal belongings. Now there are a few things that I wish I had kept a little longer.

Another thing that was particularly painful during this period was when people would say, "Remember the good memories." What they did not understand was that those memories tortured me as much as the sad ones. When you miss someone, any memory of them is an agony.

was a matter between only her and God."

While your sense of humor had a new slant to it, Katie, I must confess I felt relieved hearing Sister Regina sounding so perfectly calm and understanding. Oh, I almost forgot to tell you, Katie, when I started to say a quivering goodbye, Sister added, "Oh, and Mary Jane, for the record, your Katie is as good as any nun."

Love,

Mom

chapter *Ten*

I said to my soul, be still and wait without hope,
For hope would be hope of the wrong thing; wait without Love,
For love would be love of the wrong thing; there is yet faith,
But the faith and the hope and the love are all in the waiting.
Wait without thought, for you are not ready for thought:
So, the darkness will be the light, and the stillness, the dancing.

~T.S.ELIOT~

Katie's essence was a part of my being no matter where I looked; no matter where I went. Katie was an inextinguishable light. I didn't know how to accept her absence. So I needed to share my feelings out loud about her with a compassionate, introspective person, someone who would help me take my grief outside myself and call it what it is, "mourning." Fortunately, there are people in my life with whom I can speak about my pain and sorrow, and Dr. Alexander McCurdy III is one of them.

November 22, 1999
Dear Katie,

Hi Sweetheart, I went to see Alex today. He sent me a note of condolence; it arrived on your birthday, so synchronistic, but until today I wasn't ready to talk. When I walked through his doorway I said, "Alex, I'm here more for your spiritual guidance as a minister than because of your profession as a Jungian analyst." He nodded his head in response. After I sat down I asked him outright, "Alex, how will I ever survive without Katie? How can I possibly go on?"

He told me to remember the good things that I treasured about you, Katie, like when you won that award from the Archdiocese of Philadelphia and one thousand people stood clapping, cheering, and crying for you. He told me to remember your winning the St. Julie Billiart Award at Notre Dame de Namur - with the entire student body present - because your life contributed to the recognition of God in all creation and because of your tireless devotion to help others. Alex reminded me that it was your peers who voted you a model of faith and optimism, integrity and unselfish dedication! He asked me to remember that an annual award would be given to the graduate of your old grammar school, St. Monica's in Berwyn, who most exemplified your courage and goodness. Yes, but those wonderful memories hurt but I realized what Alex was trying to do.

He told me, "Mary Jane, our bodies break down but not our souls, for they never die. You must remember that your Katie has gone on to bigger and better things."

When my time to leave arrived, I stood up. As I moved pensively toward the door I looked back over my shoulder. That's when Alex gently smiled and reiterated, "Remember Mary Jane, your Katie has been transformed - you can do no less."

Love,
Mom

~Looking Back Reflections ~

Because I respected Alex, I very much took his advice to heart. He told me not to focus on the time apart from Katie. It was probably the single most important piece of advice that anyone offered to me. And for whatever reason it had the effect of blurring a time line between Katie and me. During this period I also came to believe that while I may never feel quite as joyful again, I may be able to feel some moments of great joy.

When I awoke this morning, I asked God, "Why am I still here?" Is this survivor's guilt? No, I feel no guilt, I just feel overwhelming grief. When Katie was still here, our son Richard often called and told me he felt as though he should be living in a cardboard box. I knew what he meant because serious illness to one part of a close family is illness to the entire. When Katie suffered, we all suffered, for indeed none of us felt worthy of a life with Katie's life so radically compromised. I think many people feel like that.

November 24, 1999
Dear Katie,

Alex analyzed a dream for me today. It was about a twelve year old boy who ignored me. Alex said, "When Jesus was twelve years old, his mother Mary became distressed because she couldn't locate Him." Alex told me he thought you were like the twelve year old Jesus who, when lost to his Mother, said He had to be about His Father's business. Alex said I must keep up with you now, Sweetheart, because you are about other business and I must be about mine. I felt encouraged hearing that about you because, quite frankly, Alex is not just an analyst he is a minister and they work directly for God!

Come to think of it, maybe we all work directly for God.

Love,
Mom

Katie's spirit is not in Calvary Cemetery, it is with God, me and everyone who loved her. Nevertheless, I know that I am lost right now. We made it through Thanksgiving. We did not cook our traditional rutabagas because they were Katie's favorites and the aromas would have been too much. Survival is the name of the game.

November 26, 1999
Dear Katie,

Your father and I talk about the terrible things you endured and we weep. Nothing comforts either one of us these holidays. I rarely go to the cemetery because I know that you are not there. And when I go and I see your name next to that angel and the Celtic cross on the stone, well, I just want to throw myself down on the ground and stay there. Not everyone likes going to cemeteries. People need to do whatever comforts them.

We went to bed early tonight, just exhausted. An hour later your father bolted upright, "Mary, Katie was here."

"She was here?"

"Yes."

"Were you dreaming, Dick?"

"No. It was like a dream but much more intense." My God, this doesn't sound like your scientific father, does it, Katie? I asked him to tell me about the experience. He said he sat on your bed when suddenly you walked in and sat down beside him. He said you looked well and healthy; that your hair was long and beautiful. He said you and he held hands. "How are you, Katie? Where are you?" he asked.

"Dad, I'm fine. I just have a few more things to do before I move on." You told your father that there was a person in New York who needed your help, and that your brother needed some help, too. "Mary Jane, this was so real. Katie came back to tell us that she is okay; that she has moved to a higher spiritual level." I was stunned hearing about your dad's sacrosanct visitation and his feelings about it, Katie, and while I felt happy for him, seeing you, talking with you, I felt sad for me because you hadn't come to visit me.

Love,
Mom

I know I will never get over Katie's death, because as Anne Finger once said, "Part of getting over it is knowing that you will never get over it."

November 27, 1999
Dear Katie,

I saw Alex McCurdy again today; I wanted his opinion about you and your dad's conversation. He told me, "Mary Jane, allow yourself to realize that Katie has moved on. The visitation to Dick confirms it." To which I responded,

"But Alex, I feel so sad that Katie didn't come to me."

"Mary Jane," Alex gently responded, "By coming to Dick, Katie did come to you."

Love,
Mom

I don't want to get out of bed but I do, every day I do. Right now that is goal enough. I have made a vow to be courageous and right now just putting my feet down on the floor is courageous. I know Katie's death was not God punishing me. I know, too, that death is not selective: rich, poor, black, white, famous, ordinary, Catholic, Protestant, Hindu, Muslim, Jewish, it really does not matter because when God calls us home, we go. That's it. When Katie's spirit left I didn't know how I was going to make it or even if I wanted to make it. Nevertheless, I got out of bed every single day. I figured, at least I was fortunate enough to have a bed and a loaf of bread under each arm, too.

November 28, 1999
Dear Katie,

Your mom is like a poor old bag lady, wandering around in my rummage sale of a mind piled high with lost goods, relinquished hopes and vanquished dreams. Great grief does that to people. Dismantling sorrow does that to parents after the death of their child. Most days I'm like an old dog, Katie, emaciated and sick, who wanders off somewhere just to be alone.

Honestly, dear Heart, nothing seems right and everything seems wrong. The world's heart ticks on; mine is barely audible. Guess I feel like running away again, Katie. Like a spoiled and sad child; as a little kid "misses the unsaid goodnight" as Robert Frost once said, "and falls asleep with a heartache," I reach over to my night stand and turn out the light with a prayer on my lips for you and for your poor father, brother, sister-in-law and mother too.

Love,
Mom

Grief is exhausting. Grief is the feeling which remains when we go through a loss. Grieving is the process of recognizing and acknowledging the loss. It is a natural response to the loss. When we allow ourselves to grieve we bring forward that loss into the rest of our life making it part of our life. That is a healthy choice.

People don't always know how to be with someone who has lost a child. I think it frightens them because if it happened to me it could happen to them. Mothers don't have to tell me I'm their worst nightmare; I know I am because I'm living my worst nightmare. I rarely talk about my sorrow or about missing Katie except with Dick because, quite frankly, it really doesn't help and people don't know what to say anyway. Or they say something that sounds insincere or is just plain stupid. Is it because they haven't experienced a loss of that depth so they can't identify? I'm not certain. A well-intentioned person might say, "Oh God never gives us more than we can handle." That's not helpful advice and it's not always true. In my line of work I've seen plenty of people be unable to handle what they've been given.

Insensitive remarks just don't help the suffering. But please understand that saying nothing is just as hurtful. I had lunch with a woman who did not know me well and when she asked me if I had children and I responded, as I normally do, "yes one living and one deceased," she changed the subject to a vacation she was planning. When Dick called to inform his parents of Katie's death, he was met with silence except to ask what time the services were and was there a chair for them to sit on at the viewing. His parents never did make it to the viewing.

November 29, 1999
Dear Katie,

Elie Wiesel, whose entire family was killed in the Holocaust, once remarked that "the opposite of life is not death, it's indifference." Today I attended a baby shower for an old friend of yours. I sat next to a woman whose son had died.

On the surface we had two major things in common: the loss of a child and we were both painters. As we dined she looked inquisitively at me then remarked, "You had a child that died; didn't I hear that about you?"

It was so soon after your death, Sweetheart, and such an odd and insensitive way to inquire. When I finally sputtered a few words about you, her only response to me was, "Oh, your loss is fresh; mine is well, old - three years ago." In a voice barely above a whisper, I inquired, "Oh, how are you managing with the loss of your son?" She picked up her napkin and slowly wiped her lips before answering nonchalantly,

"How am I doing? Why, I'm completely over it." Then she proceeded to take a bite of her sandwich as though the topic at hand had been about the temperature of the room.

Finishing my cup of tea, I quietly took my leave and said a prayer for the poor soul married to her.

Love,
Mom

November 30, 1999
Dear Katie,

When I began writing, I told our friend Sarah Ban Breathnach how much you had enjoyed her book *Simple Abundance*. I told her also how I would never be the writer that she is. Her kind response was that I wasn't supposed to be; I was supposed to be the writer that I am. Wasn't that a beautiful thing to say, Katie? As I cried softly she consoled, "Remember, M.J., you loved your Katie into full being." Her words resonated within a deep part of me because I realized you, Katie, had loved me into full being, too.

~Looking Back Reflections ~

When I think about what I really needed at this time I would have to say that I needed someone to hold my hand and give me a hug. I needed someone to say something wonderful about Katie. I needed to hear someone say her name out loud. I also needed someone to tell me that while I would never be the same again that I would make it.

Love,
Mom

December 1, 1999
Dear Katie,

Carl Jung once wrote that we cannot live the afternoon of our life in the same manner that we lived the morning of our life. He believed that what was great in the morning of our life will be little in the evening of our life. And what in the morning was true will be in the evening have become a lie. It is a strong message to me, Katie. I must rethink so many things about how to live my life now.

And it is not just your mother that is in this situation of how to live my life after a blow to the soul. When anyone of us is suffering from a big loss, we all have to reevaluate how we are going to live our life again just as you did when you were handed a brain tumor diagnosis. You know, Katie, I had a plan to love you physically well and out of a sick bed. However, restoring you to full health and wellness was just not in God's plan. Nevertheless, I think that I really did make you feel completely loved every second of every day which, when you think about it, really was just another way to "love you well."

Yes, Katie, the end of my life's morning is complete: you are with God and Rich is with Caroline. Rais-

---

~Looking Back Reflections ~

I once read that when St. Francis died an exaltation of singing larks came down low and whirled about over his monk cell. St. Francis of Assisi was called "God's fool." I think that title went beyond his holiness. I think it was about the life that he lived. So, let us live our life with our end in mind. Let us all be fools for God. Let us all pray to be ready for the singing larks over our cells.

---

ing you both was my single best contribution to this world. Now, in the afternoon of my life, it will be different and with God's help and your ever present spirit, it will be meaningful, too. I will discover my second best contribution to this world.

Love,
Mom

December 2, 1999
Dear Katie,

Your dad and I are beginning again. We are at the beach for a few days. It is cold but lovely. I continue to write in my journal. I am reaching for the pen, instead of self-pity. It's a good thing.

Love,
Mom

When someone you dearly love dies, you let yourself think that they are sleeping. When you take a nap or go to bed, your loss is asleep. When you wake up, the pain is there fresh and raw. You are often confused and disoriented. Some days I didn't recognize myself in the mirror when I awoke. Mornings can be particularly rough after a traumatic loss. But get up, dear Friend. Put your feet down on the floor. It is a good goal and it is enough.

December 3, 1999
Dear Katie,

I received a note from Sister Regina with an enclosure written by Dietrich Bonhoeffer, the German Lutheran theologian who refused submission to Hitler's cruel domination. His words brought me some solace because they make sense:

Nothing can make up for the absence of someone whom we love and it would be wrong to try to find a substitute. That sounds very hard at first, but at the same time it is a great consolation, for the gap, as long as it remains unfilled, preserves the bond between us. It is nonsense to say that God fills the gap; He doesn't fill it, but on the contrary, He keeps it empty and so helps us keep alive our former communion with each other, even at the cost of pain.

Yes Katie, the bond between us is indissolvable. One could ask any mother if that bond ever goes away regardless of the circumstances of parting. And I, like all good mothers, would say that the bond doesn't go away. Never, ever goes away. Because it's not supposed to.

Love,
Mom

The only way to avoid loss is to avoid attachment. Who would want to do that? Yet, there is a cost to that attachment, to that love, should it leave. Death or serious illness changes the equilibrium of a family. Relationships are altered for better or for worse, rising to greater heights or sinking to lower depths. Undoubtedly the life each family member once knew is gone forever; that is just the way it goes in our fluid lives. That is part of our struggle.

If we can appreciate that the ill person offered us a new view of ourselves, a kinder, sweeter version of

---

~Looking Back Reflections ~

This was the time after Katie's death when I realized that pain would forever be a part of my life and to stop fighting it. It felt as if pain were almost a real person, a fellow traveler. It was then that I stopped trying to make my pain "go away." I accepted what seemed to be true for me: that the longer we live the more losses we will have in front of us. That's just the way it goes.

who we have become, we will feel good about ourselves and that
is always a marvelous gift. In our family, Katie's care required
the best of Caroline, Rich, Dick and me. That we did our absolute
best offers consolation. We rest assured that individually and as
a family we continually focused on making Katie feel protected,
respected and deeply loved. Our Katie's ongoing smiles told us
that we had succeeded.

December 4, 1999
Dear Katie,

You embraced your love of life and your fate. I
will do no less and you, dear Katie, will help me. Some
people have said, "Katie Brant lost her battle to cancer."
I don't hold that attitude because it implies defeat and
you were a winner every step of the way. Yes of course I
realize that you and we didn't receive our most prayed-
for miracle: your complete or even partial recovery, but
our plan isn't always God's design. It's devastatingly difficult to accept the will of God here, Katie, but we must
if we are to call ourselves believers and I am a believer.

I am proud of our family, Sweetheart. We lived our
lives backwards with you. We never pretended we lacked
courage during your decade-long illness; because your

plight taught us that we had enormous courage. Mind you, I said enormous - not perfect. Inside we were often afraid but we kept moving forward anyway because you were our light in the dark. You were our role model for courage, Katie.

Yes, dear Heart, you helped us believe that a family can work from its strengths.

Love,
Mom

~Looking Back Reflections ~

As I look back on all the years we took care of Katie I don't look back with regret. Somewhere along the way I realized that the conscious decision to be the best mom I could be might have lasting effects for the rest of my life. It turned out to be one of the most important decisions that I would ever make. I lived my life backwards and thanks to Katie, she gave us a forum and made it easy to see the best in ourselves.

Katie's circumstances gave her and us two choices: be courageous or don't be courageous. With Katie as our leader, we never even considered the latter. Some people say there are no more heroes. They're wrong. I've known many heroes and most are children.

Children who are sick yet smile. Children who march into surgery. Children who sit for hours waiting for chemotherapy, radiation or their next MRI. Children who miss Christmas, Chanukah, Thanksgiving and their birthday because they are in a hospital. Children like little Alex Scott, who while having cancer herself, opened up a lemonade stand at age four (with the help of her parents) to help other kids. It has become a tremendous foundation.

These brave kids are the heroes. These wonderful, beautiful children suffer so many losses: they lose their hair again and again; they lose time in their lives because treatment regimes steal it; they often lose the ability to have a biological child because the drugs necessary for survival cause infertility. And most devastating of all, many children lose their innocent, barely lived lives when death arrives early. These children are heroic but it's not just the kids with cancer, there are many debilitating illnesses children suffer and sometimes die from. These precious little ones teach us the real meaning of valor. Katie always said that, though she never included herself in that group of heroes - but everyone else did.

December 5, 1999
Dear Katie,

There is a young boy poet named Mattie Stepanek. He has a rare form of muscular dystrophy. Three older siblings have died from it. His mother also has the disease. God help her but what an amazing child she has raised. Mattie is so inspiring and sweet. He wrote "Thank you God not just for life but for our journey through life." Yes, the journey, even for the very sad parts of our journey.

Your father and I try to help one another along this broken and harrowing path. Sometimes we succeed; sometimes we fail. Parents whose children die grieve in different ways, at different speeds, with different tools.

Your dad and I are trying to pick up our lives but we are also not used to being together without our children around. That part of our relationship many empty nesters go through. Let's face it, people who enjoy parenting will feel a great loss when the kids leave and how could they not, right Sweetheart?

Love,
Mom

I entertained an angel. One day, out of nowhere, Katie announced, "Mom, people really like reading your letters. Why don't you write a book! Call Caryn Karmatz-Rudy; she will help you!" Katie was my angel. She planted the first seed in me to write. My friend Lennie was my other advocate to write. Would I have written without their nudges? I am not certain.

~Looking Back Reflections ~

This time with Dick has afforded me an opportunity to see how easy it would be to put every sad feeling I have about anything and everything onto the loss of Katie. That would be most unfair. Life is stressful just standing by itself, even before factoring in the loss of Katie, so I work very hard at not mixing regular life stress in with Katie's death.

But as I journal I have discovered that Anne Sexton was right when she wrote that books are "People who do not leave." I think books are also the grownup's version of the thumb for sucking because well chosen words comfort the broken hearted. Writing down words comforted me plus the exercise also helped me to identify the additional losses I attached to Katie: her companionship, her affection and intelligence, and all her glorious fun. There has also been a surprise additional gift that came as a bonus for writing. By discovering what I miss, I have uncovered what I need to be happy; what I need in my life to have a life. Writing to Katie is giving me back my life.

December 8, 1999
Dear Katie,

Larry Kirshbaum, Chairman of Warner Books and your top boss, called this morning. He asked me how I can stand you not being here. I told him I couldn't stand it. I also thanked him for supporting your cause-related marketing endeavors. He told me how he loved when you would just burst into his office with all kinds of ideas bubbling out of you. He said that he loved you.

"I know, Larry, I know. Some of us have entertained angels unaware," was all that I could say. Then we just sighed and cried together.

Love,
Mom

Our friend, Frank Kirk, who delivered one of Katie's eulogies, underwent emergency multiple-by-pass surgery. I dashed to our Katie's closet, picked out one of the few silk scarves that I had not yet given away, and headed to the hospital. I figured Frank could put it in view and be fortified by her spiritual presence.

December 9, 1999
Dear Katie,

I visited Frank Kirk in the hospital and gave him one of your scarves. Without speaking, he tied it to the footboard of his bed. For a long silent moment we stared at one another, undoubtedly both thinking about you. Frank spoke first, "M.J., before anesthesia, the last person's face I saw was Katie's. I knew then, that one way or the other, I would be okay." Blinking back my tears I confided,

"I'm happy for you, Frank, but honestly? I'm jealous, too, because Katie still hasn't come to me." With an expression of sweet surrender on his handsome Irish face he looked at me and said, straight out,

"Well, M.J., maybe I just needed Katie more than you did."

Love,
Mom

chapter *Eleven*

When one door of happiness closes, another opens;
but often we look so long at the closed door
that we do not see the one which has been opened for us.

~HELEN KELLER~

The closed door will always be there. Across the hall is another door and it is already open. It is not easy to walk through it because old loyalties surface in question form as, "If I walk into a new life does that mean that I stopped loving what I left behind?"

No, it means you are honoring that which must be left to rest in peace.

December 12, 1999
Dear Katie,

Back in the late summer we visited Richard and Caroline in Virginia. They gave us a tour of their beautiful new brick town home. When we walked into a small bedroom, Caroline asked me, "Do you like this room, M.J.?"

"Yes, Caroline," I responded, "it is a lovely room."

"Here," she said as she handed me a little present.

"It looks like a book," I replied, tearing off the paper. *So You're Going to be Grandparents* was its title. It registered, I looked up; your brother and Caroline were smiling.

"Caroline, are you pregnant?"

"Yes, M.J., I am." Dick was smiling and I was crying, of course I was, Katie. My mother's heart was bursting with joy for them, for all of us, in every fractured part of it. These were enormous events to contain simultaneously: your death and the expected birth of our first grandchild – an agony and an ecstasy, the seen world and the unseen world. I cannot imagine how I will ever manage these two separate realities. No wonder Carl Jung said that life is a luminous pause between two great mysteries which yet are one. Birth, death, they are more than a mind can wrap itself around.

Katie, I believe I'm being invited to the next part of my journey.

Love,
Mom

I am trying to stay focused on the pregnancy but my memories of Katie are competing. It is confusing and painful.

December 14, 1999
Dear Katie,

The spiritual aspects of life differ dramatically from the temporal. The spiritual is abstract; the temporal concrete. You are in the spiritual realm now, Sweetheart, and the new baby is in the temporal. I loved you for twenty-eight years and I have not yet met the new child. Your death is still bigger than the idea of being a grandmother because every time I remember that I won't see you again on this earth, I feel so upset. It is a moment I can't even begin to describe. Did Dante ever really describe hell? And those of us left behind, like your mother, where do we look for solace? Where do we look for consolation? I don't have the answer to that right now and you know how your mom loves to have the answer.

Love,
Mom

~Looking Back Reflections ~

As I look at what I have learned during this time I realize that most situations are rarely perfect. Caroline and Rich's pregnancy is already teaching me something for myself and even for my clients who often struggle with wanting things to be perfect. "I'm pregnant for the fourth time and my best friend can't conceive," one shared recently. I was able to discuss the situation better thanks to "the baby on the way." Holding the pregnancy in one hand and Katie's death in the other with the tension that caused inside of me helped me to mature both emotionally and spirituality.

Nothing is perfect, nothing. It is rare and unusual when things and events even come close. It is more likely that we will have wonderful moments within ordinary days.

December 15, 1999
Dear Katie,

I would like to share with you some words of one of my favorite writers and philosophers. His name is John O'Donohue. He is from Connemara, Ireland. He seems to understand something about the mystery of birth and the mystery of death.

Something breaks within you then that will never come together again. Gone is the person whom you loved, whose face and hands and body you knew so well. This body, for the first time, is completely empty. This is very frightening and strange.... The death of a loved one is bitterly lonely. When you really love someone, you would be willing to die in their place. Yet no one can take another's place when that time comes.... The deceased literally falls out of the visible world of form and presence. At birth you appear out of nowhere, at death you disappear to nowhere.... The terrible moment of loneliness in grief comes when you realize that you will never see the deceased again. The absence of their life, the absence of their voice, face, and presence become something that, as Sylvia Plath says, begins to grow beside you like a tree.[6]

Love,
Mom

---

6 Anam Cara – p. 207-208)

I tried to distract myself from pain so that I could function. I discovered that the single most effective and concrete means for coping with pain, fear, sorrow or loss - no matter what the circumstances - was distraction.

The *Simple Abundance* Principle of Order helped me to distract myself from some pain this winter by organizing. Many people are reluctant to begin this task, to change things in the house after a love one has moved to live somewhere else, or has died. By putting order into my life, I am hoping to create an inner space that something or someone else can come into. I am hoping my space will be filled with a baby's laughter.

December 16, 1999
Dear Katie,

I find myself looking at my easel again. I squeezed my tubes of oil paint. Maybe that decluttering actually helped. I've read that most interests will return to normal, Catherine. Your dad tells me not to worry, that I'll be painting again. I love it when he tells me that; it's encouraging and it gives me hope. It's wonderful to offer someone hope.

Love,
Mom

When we have lost someone, that is all that we can think about. Rationally, I realize that Katie is free of all worldly suffering and for that I feel grateful. Nevertheless, it is lonely living in the world without my beloved daughter. It is all consuming and perfectly described by C. S. Lewis who wrote "Her absence is like the sky, spread over everything," when his beloved wife died. Even being together as a family is painful now. We look around at one another and all we see is that Katie isn't here anymore. Nobody knows if we're talking too much about Katie or not enough about her. Nobody knows how to manage this time apart from Katie or what's right anymore. "Nobody" could be my name.

December 16, 1999
Dear Katie,

I went for a manicure today, that place where we always went. The girls who work there cried seeing me walk in without you. The owner told me brusquely, "Pick a color." After I sat down she squinted at me. "You look better since daughter die, less wrinkles, skin smoother." Her remarks caused me instant vertigo. I wanted to shout out, "Give me back my wrinkles! Give me back my life!" What I really wanted was for God to give you back to me.

Love,
Mom

~Looking Back Reflections ~

I've noticed that as time moved on people asked less and less, "How are you doing?" Our society allows little time for grieving or feeling sad. Things always have to be upbeat. During this time it was difficult for me to even feel normal. I had no point of reference for what it even meant "to feel normal" which made me lonely. I think that loneliness set me up to feel afraid and wonder if I would become worse as time went on.

I have never been a big TV person but I suddenly found myself watching Oprah every day. I knew that I could count on her being there. Her mixture of joy and authenticity engaged me. I quietly realized that I was being invited back into the land of the living.

We are all making our way through this life and, as we do, we discover a sweet blessing: we will meet some good, exceptional and loving people along the journey. Katie's doctors and nurses fell into all of those categories. Neither patient nor family manages a long-term illness without their care, help and support. The love was a bonus. When I hear people using that somewhat challenging phrase, "Blood is thicker than water!" I always smile because that doesn't fit my belief system at all. I've known many people more related by love than by blood.

December 18, 1999
Dear Katie,

You adored your doctors and nurses, especially Dr. Jonathan Finlay. Well, Katie, here is some wonderful news. Your Dad, Caroline, Rich and I went with a big group to New York City for an event sponsored by The Children's Brain Tumor Foundation where Jonathan awarded your foundation's first grant of $100,000. Your surgeon and friend, Jeff Wisoff, M.D., was there, too. Jeff said you were one of his heroes. What a wonderful acknowledgment of the good work your life exemplified.

Afterward we gathered the group for dinner. There we toasted you and your foundation, Katie. Then

I handed Jonathan that little blue pillow that you had on your office door with the embroidered message, "Miracles do happen." He lowered his eyes and smiled, before telling us all that you were the little sister that he never had.

Love,
Mom

December 19, 1999
Dear Katie,

You once told me that you never wanted to be buried in the ground because you didn't want me on my knees at some grave when I could be living my life instead. But the holidays are approaching, Katie; it makes it worse for people suffering a loss. I gave in today. I decided to accept my sad feelings and I went to the cemetery. I also read a few old letters and looked at photos of us. It made me cry out to heaven, "Oh God, I must be living somebody else's life; Oh, let it be somebody else's life!" Then a thought crossed my mind: "Why did you leave me?"

Oh, please forgive me, Sweetheart, what a terrible thing to think - be with me or be with God? I am trying to cope, Katie, honestly I am. Your dad encouraged me to get back into art but I still do not feel ready to use colorful paint, so I've begun a sculpting class instead. Something new, something different. "What are you feeling, M.J.? What do you want the piece to say?" the instructor asks me. He said that my piece is powerful. I'm glad he senses that, and I actually think he recognizes that I'm sad. But Katie, does he realize I'm trying to find myself again? Trying to find my way back to the upper world?

I think he does.

Love,
Mom

Katie did not censor her dreams nor allow anyone else to. She never had the mindset of "What's the use starting this" or "I may never get well so I might as well give up now." Katie was the entrepreneur of her own life. That phrase comes from my friend, Richard Caruso, who says true

~Looking Back Reflections ~

During this period I discovered that engaging my senses helped to calm me. A new experience, such as the sculpting class, helped tremendously. Additionally, I think the creative and artistic world is overall more accepting of people's feelings.

entrepreneurs do not allow people or circumstances to thwart their personal pursuits of success. I love that premise and it certainly describes Katie for she had an entrepreneurial spirit right from childhood. It made her stand apart.

I wanted to help Katie manifest what would become her final personal definition of success: her foundation, but it was becoming physically harder because Katie was more and more exhausted. I think back on the days when she would lie on the couch, "Mom, I can barely move." So on those days we wouldn't move, we played Scrabble instead or talked.

Some days Katie just rested her head on a pillow and put her feet in my lap. Those days I kept things calm and peaceful. It made Katie's life easier to go about her business: conserving energy and getting her foundation operational. It also made my life easier to go about my business: loving, encouraging, and protecting her.

December 20, 1999
Dear Katie,

Your absence has created a space and chasm so deep within me I think I echo when I speak. I pray to God, "How will I reconcile the moments of my life in the absence of you?" Does God really think I have any courage left, Katie? The courage to live without you? Well, if God thinks I have the courage, then I have the courage.

When you were first going through your treatments and a starting sophomore at Penn you casually said to me, "Mom, I'm not afraid to die." We were holding hands and kicking the leaves down Locust Walk on campus. Then you leaned over and gave me three little butterfly kisses like you did when you were a child.

I loved you beyond love in that moment, Katie, and I couldn't fathom such fearlessness at such a tender age. I also couldn't imagine my life without you in it.

Love,
Mom

All trials force the question, who are you, really? . . . .
It's up to each of us to get very still and say, "This is who I am."

~OPRAH WINFREY, O MAGAZINE, OCTOBER, 2000~

When Katie died I forgot who I was. Now I am beginning to remember who I am. How I have responded to the circumstances of my life has defined me even if I forgot for a while. I'm not living a perfect life, or a saintly one, but I am trying to love God and do the best that I can.

December 22, 1999
Dear Katie,

I know that something inside of me is broken now, something that will never be repaired. It's true. But maybe it's not supposed to be repaired; maybe that's the way God tempts us to desire heaven more than earth. And you and I both know that while something very big is indeed broken inside of me, it is not the whole me.

Love,
Mom

I believe that every soul has a purpose here on earth. I am searching for my new purpose and I like to think the new purpose is also searching for me. Sometimes our purpose presents through an illness. I think of the late Pope John Paul II.

As a young pope, he stood commanding and robust on his skis in the Italian Alps. In 1992, after he was struck with Parkinson's Disease, we all watched him continue being the man of conviction that he always was but now in a frail and broken body. Nevertheless, he was no less convincing. No less effective. Humility and courage are as formidable as power and strength.

Pope Julius II commissioned Michelangelo, Raphael and Bramante in the early 1500's for the art and architecture that has brought millions of people to gaze, weep, and sigh throughout the centuries. This pope met his purpose. When we discover our purpose our life takes on a deeper meaning because we understand "Now I have a calling; a reason for being!"

Katie's soul invited her to help little children and she did by creating Katie's Kids for the Cure. She did not allow fear to stop her. My soul invited me to write this book to help me find myself once again. To write this book to help others to find their courage and their lost self again too. To write this book to help others recommit to their life after loss, especially after loss. This is my new purpose: to write words that help people heal.

I believe that one person can change the world. Jesus

believed it, Gandhi believed it, Buddha believed it, Nelson Mandela believes it, Oprah believes it, I believe it, and dear darling Katie believed it, too.

The transitions in life are hard. They make our life seem unrecognizable. My life is different now. Katie is no longer here and neither is Richard. I know that; I

accept that. Nevertheless, it doesn't stop me from periodically reminiscing and occasionally touching that place over my heart, reminding me where my children reside now....Reminding me that my heart shall never ever be empty even if Katie is with God and Richard is with Caroline....Reminding me that the most important thing is that they are safe and happy. For that I am so grateful because deep down that is all any mother or father really wants.

December 23, 1999
Dear Katie,

Christmas is only two days away. I'm struggling again. I have two questions for you today, Sweetheart. One, I wonder how much suffering a heart can take before it breaks apart; shatters completely into a thousand pieces. Two, is my deeper search for faith worth it?

That's when I hear you answer me back, Katie, "Maybe, Mom, ...that's where the ... stars ... come... from."

Love,
Mom

chapter Twelve

Blackberry winter,
the time when the hoarfrost
lies on the blackberry blossoms;
without this frost the berries will not set.
It is the forerunner of a rich harvest.

~MARGARET MEAD, BLACKBERRY WINTER, 1972~

Holidays are painful without the ones we love. This first Christmas without our Katie is so bad that we can barely speak, never mind sing.

December 24, 1999 – Christmas Eve
Dear Katie,

We are staying overnight at Rich and Caroline's home in Virginia. Caroline is now seven months pregnant. Our blessing before dinner was filled with remembrances of you. I thought I wouldn't be able to make it through dinner but I breathed deeply and vowed not to let my sorrow fill their new home tonight; it wouldn't be good for the baby, the mother-to-be or your brother.

It's my unspoken gift to Caroline and Richard.

Love,
Mom

December 25, 1999 – Early Christmas Morning
Dear Katie,

I sat quietly in bed this morning reminiscing about the many wonderful Christmas mornings that we shared together as a family. Your father always made them special. I thought about my mother, too, Katie. For her, Christmas was always sad; she missed my father more during the holidays. I did too, but I was just a kid; I still wanted to have fun. Maybe Mom was past all the fun. Your father was always sensitive to my feelings concerning my mother and the circling dynamics around my deceased father. "Well, I know you're probably worrying about your mother," he would say. "How about we give her a wonderful gift this Christmas? The color that helps her out with her taxes?" This was an annual ritual; and your dad always played along as if it were the first time we ever did it. It made me deliriously happy.

I shall always love your father for his generosity to my mother, Katie. It was one of the ways he helped heal my own child's heart because by being kind to my mother he was being kind to me.

Love,
Mom

December 25 - Later in the day

Dick and I left Virginia early Christmas morning. He asked me if we could visit his parents in New Jersey saying it would be good for us to be with his siblings on this first Christmas without Katie. Because I was missing her so terribly I didn't want to visit, but Dick said it would be better than being home alone. I wasn't so sure; I had a bad feeling inside.

Minutes after arriving, my father-in-law announced a family meeting to discuss something about his estate, adding authoritatively, "It's just for our children." When I asked him if he had forgotten to mention their mates he repeated, "I said, just our children." Dick said he was not going if I was not invited. A heated discussion ensued with words like, "I'm the father!" and "I'm not the boy" filling the air.

I hurried then into the kitchen where my mother-in-law stood talking with two of her grown children. I interrupted them and asked my mother-in-law to intercede in the dispute. In an indifferent tone she responded, "But Mary, how do I know my son won't eventually divorce you?"

It hurt me. It was a terrible thing to say. I was devoted to Dick and he to me; she knew that. A little while later she said she was sorry but added that if she didn't apologize I would hold it against her forever. That didn't seem like much of an apology to me.   A few family members also heard the exchange. They stared open mouthed but said nothing. That hurt me more.

Dispirited, Dick and I left soon afterwards. When I took his hand in the car, a quiet thought seeped into my heart. I felt it was Katie saying that it was her absence which carried the power over my heart, not the other family nonsense. I nodded my head in agreement and vowed to stop wishing things could be better here.

December 31, 1999
Dear Katie,

It is New Year's Eve. There will be no talk tonight about what movie to rent, what kind of dip and chips to buy. No more hearing your dad ask you, "How about a nice fire, Katie?" No more quiet moments at the end of the day when you would say, "Good job today, Mom, good job" and I always smiled and echoed back, "Good job today, Katie, good job."

Today is the last day of the year and understand-ably the saddest year of our lives. Your dad and I lis-tened to Andrea Bocelli sing 'A Time to Say Goodbye' and just as we did at Richard and Caroline's wedding, we danced and clung together.

Love,
Mom

I barely made it through January and February. I felt depressed and withdrawn but as the weather warmed up a bit in the middle of February, I began thinking more about the new life growing inside of Caroline. I thought about how life can bring us a new season unexpectedly. And a change in seasons definitely alerts us of things to come, things to be, yet nothing could have prepared our hearts for the change and wonder that occurred with the arrival of our grandson, Connor Thomas Brant, born on Leap Year Day, February 29, 2000.

February 29, 2000 Leap Year!
Dear Katie,

Your dad and I are on a cruise for my birthday and we have wonderful news! A darling child has leaped into our lives! Can there be any doubt that a baby delivered on Leap Day, February 29th, isn't destined for good fortune? Caroline and Rich believe you helped choose his soul, Katie. They believe your souls passed one another on their individual journeys, our little Pisces grandson. And, guess what, Sweetheart, they are naming the baby Connor and he has glorious red hair, just like his Aunt Katie.

Love,
Mom

March 1, 2000

Dear Katie,

I'm so upset. Connor is in intensive care. They are not sure why, only that he arrived a little over two weeks early and there could be a lung issue. We made several ship-to-shore contacts today to speak person-to-person with Rich.

Love,
Mom

March 2, 2000

Dear Katie,

Connor has a problem with his lungs. We are so concerned and helpless. I went to Mass on the ship and when I told this little Italian priest about Connor, I started crying. He touched my arm, "I will celebrate Mass each morning just for him."

Love,
Mom

March 3, 2000
Dear Katie,

The ship-to-shore communication system is down in Miami. We can't get through by phone. We will try again later. Your father is so upset; he skipped dinner and stayed in the room.

Love,
Mom

March 4, 2000
Dear Katie,

Connor is doing poorly. They have a tube in his little chest. We are five hundred miles away from any port and can't do a thing. This is a nightmare. Dear Lord, please take care of this baby for Richard and Caroline. Please, Katie, watch over him and be his guardian angel.

Love,
Mom

March 5, 2000
Dear Katie,

Connor must stay in the hospital. Caroline and Rich must go home without Connor because he needs to become stronger. It is heartbreaking for them.

Love,
Mom

March 7, 2000
Dear Katie,

Connor is better! The tube is out! We are relieved and grateful! We can't wait to get off this damn ship and see him.

Love,
Mom

March 18, 2000
Dear Katie,

Caroline and Richard have had Connor at home with them since March 8th. They wanted some alone time with him before Caroline's folks came for a few days to help out. Then it was our turn! There is no word other then "joy" to describe the feeling I had when I held Connor in my arms today. He is well, Sweetheart. He is just fine. As I looked into his adorable little face I told him that I would bring him everything I have to give and I will.

Love,
Mom

March 22, 2000
Dear Katie,

I told Lennie about Connor's arrival. I also asked her, "What if I start feeling depressed?"

"Mare, don't be a glum grandmother," she responded. It was the best advice anyone could have given to me. Not only will I not be a glum grandmother, I will be the grandmother of all grandmothers! I will teach him to paint and to write stories and he will teach me many things too! We will have a ball.

Love,
Mom

~Looking Back Reflections ~

This period after Katie's death was full of mystery and surprise for me because when I least expected it I saw a light shining under the doorway. Connor was the light for me. His presence began opening something up in me. And where my writing gave me a new purpose to live, my grandson gave me a new reason to love again.

chapter *Thirteen*

I want to go on living even after my death.

~ANNE FRANK~
THE DIARY OF A YOUNG GIRL

Connor's presence in my life has given me new energy, new ideas, and an abundance of hope. I realized that something in his spirit was prompting me to share Katie with the world. So eleven months after Katie's death, I gathered up the notebooks I had filled with letters, stories and my feelings about Katie, my life and this sorrowful last year. I realized that they were indeed the beginnings of a book. All I needed now was a sacred space in which to organize the notebooks creatively. Finding a place to write at the Jersey Shore seemed the answer.

I drove down to Ocean City with Dick. When I saw a commercial real estate advertisement with an old friend's name splashed across it I exhaled, "There's the sign." St. Benedict once said, "Whatsoever good work you undertake, pray earnestly to God that He will enable you to bring it to a successful conclusion." I called our old friends, the Dwyers, and explained what I had in mind. They generously loaned me a one-bedroom family condo for the months of June and July. Ask and ye shall receive.

March 25, 2000
Dear Katie,

William Hazlitt, the Irish Protestant, once said, "If you think you can win, you can win. Faith is necessary to victory." So when I walked into this sweet little condo and spotted the identical hand-stitched pillow with "Miracles Do Happen" written on it, the one that I had given to Doctor Finlay, my legs went weak and I started laughing. I immediately called Josh Dwyer, who worked for the company that owned the unit and who himself had a brain tumor. I wanted to tell him about the synchronicity. He started crying, "Oh, Mrs. B. I love you and I loved Katie. Please keep the pillow!"

Love,
Mom

When my first Mother's Day without Katie arrived, Rich, Caroline, Connor and Dick helped me to stay in my own skin. This was also Caroline's first official Mother's Day and I didn't want to ruin it for her by making the day about me. Connor clearly helped by being my adorable distraction. He's such a pretty baby with his red fluffy hair, so soft and shiny. He smiles all the time now and he has completely captured my heart. Truthfully, I'm less afraid to love him now - an understandable and natural reaction to a great and permanent loss.

May 13. 2000
Dear Katie,

Rich invited me to go on a walk today. He was wonderful and I can always be myself, which comforts me. He asked me, "Mom, are you doing all right?" My honest response was that seeing him, Caroline, and the baby helps me be able to do all right. I told him how comforting it is to hold Connor and see his adorable little face. Rich nodded his head and hugged my shoulder. He knew we were also talking about you, Katie. He knows it is hard for me now without you, because it is hard for him now without you, his big sister, Katie. Richard said he loves being a dad. How Connor makes every day feel like a party. He told me that he and Caroline sometimes call him "The Con Man." Undoubtedly he has some of his Grandmom M.J. in him.

After everyone left, your Dad poured me a glass of wine and we sat and talked. He reminded me that you had died in peace, Katie. He said he believed you drew from a mystical bond of love which you and I shared. That somehow my love for you kept you here much longer than was humanly possible. I think that was the most beautiful thing your father has ever said to me, Katie, and it touched me deeply.

And while actions may speak louder than words for some people, I know that I need both.

Love,
Mom

Last night I dreamed about Katie. The feeling tone of the dream was one of protection. There was a baby in the dream that Katie wanted to hold - she didn't want to see the infant hurt. Then she handed the baby over to me, "Mom, please protect it." The baby was hungry. I looked around and saw a happy nursing mother enter the room. I went up to her, smiled and handed her the baby. She held it close.

May 24, 2000
Dear Katie,

I had a dream that I felt was important about the managing of your foundation, your waking, personal life's dream which you always called "your baby." There was a nursing mother in the dream. Caroline is a nursing mother. You know, Katie, from the start Caroline was always respectful that you, only you, had founded Katie's Kids for the Cure. Did you know, Sweetheart, that days before you died, as I sat at your desk sorting through mounds of paper work, checks and letters written to you related to your foundation, I thought to myself, "What in the name of all that's good and holy am I going to do with this foundation?" I was completely overwhelmed and out of my league. Katie's Kids for the Cure was everything to you but I also knew I'm a psychotherapist, not a CEO of a children's fund. The details of continuing your dream made me feel like putting my head down on the desk and going to sleep for a million years.

Just then Caroline entered the room, sat down on the floor next to my chair and offered - in that very moment - to assume responsibility for your foundation. I remember her presence and her words filling me with such profound relief, such admiration and affection that I began crying. "M.J." she said, "My dream has always been to run a non-profit. It will make me happy to manage Katie's foundation."

So, darling Girl, Katie's Kids for the Cure has an incredible Earth Mother and that's Caroline Toedtman Brant. Your foundation also has a beautiful Heavenly Mother, and that's you, dear Katie.

Love,
Mom

A father who turns his tender love
towards a most virtuous, most reverend daughter
cannot deny himself the full expression of his loss at her
departure....A maiden so good and holy will make her way
straight to the Lord God, and pray for you there....

~SIGNOR G. BOCCHINERI~
TO GALILEO ON THE DEATH OF HIS DAUGHTER, 1633

Dick's sorrow at Katie's leaving is, respectfully, indescribable. I am the most privileged person to share in his grief. Dick
was Katie's hero, a status that didn't happen overnight: it took
years. He was just twenty-five when Katie was born; and almost
twenty-seven when Richard arrived. I would like to share a little
bit about the father Dick was. He frequently read to the children,
particularly animal books where he croaked, barked, mooed and
quacked every sound from A to Z. On Saturday mornings he
faithfully took the kids on errands and to the park which gave
me much needed time for my undergraduate degree studies
because when Dick and I married, I had only twenty-one credits toward my degree. When Richard was a year and a half old,
I returned to night school and Dick always pitched in to help me
get through.

Dick was an involved father: he went to the soccer games,
basketball games, baseball games, recitals and he cared about all
the proms. He handled many of the talks about what was "really"
important, like honoring a commitment, doing hard work, and
having integrity. He demonstrated saintly patience during all
the times Katie missed her curfew "again" and kept clearing her
throat and touching her nose when she was trying to get away
with something. Dick was never afraid to address boy issues with
Katie, with many talks about sex and how hickies don't look nice
no matter how they happened. There was also "the fatherly con-

versation" he had with one serious boyfriend whom he asked the poignant question, "What are your intentions?" that Katie never minded and, in fact, expected and appreciated.

Dick was a sensitive father. When Richard was little and became emotional, Dick helped him work it through just by telling him to take a nice slow breath and tell his dad what was going on. Dick was an unselfish father, evident from all the days, weeks, months and years he set aside caring for his children when they needed him, especially Katie as an adult child due to the demands of her illness. Evident from each emergency room visit, on a second's notice, in New York, Connecticut, and Philadelphia. Evident each time he pushed Katie in the wheelchair from the emergency room back to the apartment in New York at 1:30 a.m. on many occasions too numerous to mention and mentioning them would embarrass him anyway.

Dick was a fun father. On all the camping trips we took with the kids and on all the boats we fished in. On all of the trips up to Lake George, New York, where we stayed in that little cabin and he taught the children how to swim, cajoling Richard gently and daily to get his 'whole' face wet. On all of the nights during Katie's illness when he ran out to Blockbuster for yet 'another Saturday night at home' when we knew that was where we would be and he made it such fun for us. On all the adventures on that big boat he bought so that Katie would have something fun to do and look forward to no matter how big that proverbial "hole in the sea" became. And finally with all of the board and card games he played with the kids even after he lost, one more time.

Dick was a loveable father. Evident all the times he told the children that he loved them and accepted their love in return. Evident all the times he stayed with Richard to make him do his homework because he knew it would help Rich out in the world even if it made him 'the bad cop.' Evident every night he escorted Katie up our long flight of stairs before bed, her arm through his for stability.

Dick had the ability to be a father when it would have been easier to be a friend, and the flexibility to be a friend when it would have been easier to hide behind the role of father. With the hundreds of hugs, kisses and encouraging words he poured out to help Katie and Richard manifest their every gift. Indeed, my husband Dick was and is the father that every kid wishes they had.

June 18, 2000
Dear Katie,

It's Father's Day and it's a sad day for yours. Taking care of you and Richard was something your dad not only liked, but loved doing. Being a father to you and your brother has been his greatest joy and fulfillment. As Khalil Gibran said, "When you are sorrowful look again in your heart, and you shall see that in truth you are weeping for that which has been your delight." Yes Katie, your brother Rich was your dad's joy. And you, dear Katie, were his delight.

Love,
Mom

We took Katie to Mass on those Sundays she felt well enough to go. On one occasion I introduced her to a priest friend of mine, Father Michael Bielecki. Because Katie had a burning desire to discuss theological issues, this priest, whose background included having lived and studied in Rome for twelve years, became her fertile sounding board. After his visits he would leave shaking his head at Katie's intelligence and insight; he would also be drying his eyes and sighing at her condition.

Katie never backed down from any discussion with Father Michael regardless of any taboos attached to it. Questioning dogma was as comfortable for her as breathing in and breathing out. I feel terrific about that.

~Looking Back Reflections ~

*This period offered me a breathing space to think about my children and how we raised them. I realized that Dick and I were a parent team and our home operated as an open family system which meant no topic was off limits ***

It was natural that Katie and Richard learned to navigate differences in opinions given that their parents had opposite personalities in many ways. Dick kept us grounded and I kept us open. I wanted our kids to fly like that eagle and open their wings to capture every new idea. Dick wanted to make sure they got a degree and a job. I think that combination worked to give our children the most important gift that a parent can bestow: self-confidence.

*** Scarf, Maggie, Life Inside the Family, 1995.*

June 19, 2000
Dear Katie,

I remember the day you met Father Michael. "Father, I'm a lot of trouble for my mom and dad these days," you said, while we stood in the back of church. I swallowed hard that morning, trying to stop myself from crying. Then gently, Father Michael smiled and responded, "Katie, it gives your mother and father an opportunity to practice charity."

Yes, dear Katie, it was the quintessential privilege to demonstrate our love for you, my daughter who had the temperamental qualities of St. Therese of Lisieux, that little French Carmelite nun who once said, "You want a means for reaching perfection? I know of only one: Love." You could have said that, Katie, but you would have winked and added, "And cause-related marketing."

Love,
Mom

Yes, reflecting on my life this last year has made me realize what an arduous road Dick and I have traveled. Left to my own devices and to an inflated sense of my own 'authority,' I could have failed miserably at marriage. Thankfully, my husband doesn't overreact to my deafening threats, frequent demands and childish temper tantrums. People who know him call him Saint Richard - being married to me has offered him that opportunity.

Certainly not every marriage lasts forever; some were never meant to. Many couples, despite pure intensions, end up divorcing. Dick and I have stopped and started many marriages within our present one. Let me explain what I mean by that. At a conference in Ireland, a senior analyst from New England mentioned to our group how he and his wife "had had many marriages." Everyone laughed. Then he added, "but with each other." I was intrigued.

When Dick and I first married, I was happily pregnant in three months. Katie arrived before our first anniversary so our "First Marriage" always felt about having a family to me. We were a couple, but one "expecting" a child, so the upcoming birth seemed more about the family to me and less about us as a couple. We were also a happy family. I adored every wonderful year of it.

After Katie was diagnosed with cancer, Dick and I struggled terribly because our original family construct was dramatically threatened and forever changed. The family of origin issues flooded our little family well and the water was never the same. I believe Katie's brain tumor diagnosis literally began our "Second Marriage." For close to one year this second marriage was like a drowning person that no one knew how to save. Neither one of us had experience with anything like it before. I was not convinced we could make it. Being in our early forties didn't help either, because psychologically most couples – even without the stress of a seriously sick child - will have their family of origin issues surface during this developmental stage. Indeed the unconscious will make itself visible through the father and mother complexes, both positive and negative, that each partner carries within their psychic inner worlds. It is predictable.

"Complexes are always more or less unconscious; they are charged with energy and operate autonomously. Although usually activated by an event in the present, the psyche operates analogously, saying in effect, 'When have I been here before?' The current stimulus may be only remotely similar to something that happened in the past, but if the situation is emotionally analogous, then the historically occasioned response is triggered." [7] Most of us have emotionally charged responses to sex, money or authority issues. They are linked to our original family histories.

---

7 Hollis, *The Middle Passage: From Misery to Meaning in Midlife*,
   p. 13

Our "Third Marriage" began when Katie started looking better and getting better. With each improved MRI and doctor report, I felt Dick's and my spirits lift. It was during this period that we bought a condo at the shore that I wallpapered and bought new dishes for. Our intimacy returned and deepened. The hope and fun and trust returned. We focused on what we enjoyed about one another and it transported us back to our honeymoon period. I felt so grateful because we acted like newlyweds in every way so I love remembering this "Third Marriage."

Our "Fourth Marriage" was hard but beautiful. Katie had relapsed twice but Dick and I did not repeat our old dysfunctional patterns. We integrated the lessons learned from the "Second Marriage" and this time we did things right. During this period we had many physical and emotional demands: barely settled into the Connecticut house with all of that hope, Dick with a new job, with my starting up a new practice, to spending half of our time in New York City hospitals. As a couple I think we did an amazing job. When we returned to Philadelphia we again had great hopes that all would be well. Dick always believed that Katie would get well. I wanted to believe, but I always felt the underlying possibility that she might not. As you all know by now, our precious Katie did not return to health and we had to give her back to God.

Our "Fifth Marriage" has been about living as a couple after Katie's death. It has been about survival, clinging together, trying to make some sense out of what life has handed us individually and as a couple. Dick literally was cut off at the knees with a double knee replacement which resurrected my fears of "would we ever be in the sunshine again?" for it was a brutal surgery and I knew and he knew that he could not have made it through without me. But that is what committed couples do for one another, they step right up to the plate, grab that bat, and hit a few balls clean out of the park.

Dick and I are individually strong people and when we stay individuated we are a fantastic team. Being joined at the hip does not work for us. He does not define me nor I him. I also will not back down when I know we are having "a breach birth" of something new, or *Something More* as my friend Sarah would say. I think a little pain and patience, mixed together, more often than not does reward a couple. But the single most wonderful experience we now share in the Fifth Marriage is being grandparents.

Our "Sixth Marriage" began recently. We are now about our future. It is about what makes Dick individually happy; me individually happy and finding how we define our goals as a team while at the same time allowing those lovely spaces, those delicate places within our own souls, to breathe and breathe deeply. Our couple agenda is presently still in embryo but I know that this sixth marriage won't be boring given how much I adore my husband's sense of humor. Seriously, he makes me laugh every day; calls me "The Mouthy One," and says he needs a gun and a whip to approach me during a fight. With those kinds of one-liners, it's easy to see that when I get mad at him, I quickly get glad.

After our dear Katie's death we needed "amazing grace" to pick up our life again. God must have thought us worthy because it was granted. It's not easy for us to manage this soul agony as a couple, not easy at all. We bereaved parents must understand that our mate is also suffering but may be mourning his or her loss differently, oftentimes privately, but grieving nevertheless. We bereaved parents need to be patient and kind first with ourselves and second with one another but especially we need to remind one another that no one, absolutely no one, loved their precious child from beginning to end more than we did.

June 30, 2000
Dear Katie,

Your father's character is so full of integrity that I marvel at my luck in having found him in this broken world so full of projection and disappointment. I know you worried about the stress of your illness on our relationship. But even if you had never had a diagnosis,

Katie, your father and I were a typical example of the mid-life couple who would have struggled with unfinished business anyway, believe me. And with the two circumstances colliding together simultaneously, we really needed more than a dollop of grace to survive.

Love,
Mom

Our first year without Katie has ended. I must confide that after one year, loss does not disappear or even diminish; it merely plunges itself deeper within the heart and becomes part of the mourner's body experience. Yes, dear Reader, I accept the separation and loss of my daughter. I accept it as nature's way and God's will. I also focus on the word "loss" here because it implies "find" - a happy rejoicing image of Katie and me finding one another again.

My daughter's death amplified one of my deepest belief systems: that our children are not truly ours. We think they are, but they are not. They are God's children and He lends them to us - sometimes for a long time; sometimes for a short time. I respect that my way may not be your way, dear Reader. I'm finding my path given my family history, spiritual values, strengths and weaknesses. "Meaning arises even out of the places of great suffering," James Hollis, Ph.D. writes in *Creating a Life*. Yes, it clearly does and we don't always know what the meaning will be. Recently a new friend of mine mentioned that my book was like having a magic wand. I told her, "Oh, Sarah gave Katie a magic wand on the day she told Katie that she was dedicating *Something More* to her." My friend responded, "It's yours now, M.J. Katie wants you to have it. It's the baton and she has passed it onto you. Put the magic wand in your office so that you can see it every day."

July 10, 2000
Dear Katie,

Today is your anniversary. It has been a sad and lonely year since I kissed you good-bye. It is unfathomable that this broken heart still beats at all. I think God had something to do with it. God and precious Connor.

I do believe you are now at rest, Katie. At peace with the angels, the saints and all those souls who have gone before us. You asked me once to focus on your victories. I am because it feels right to do that and I know that it also makes you happy. And when my time comes to die, I hope my loved ones here honor me in that same way, too. Life is a gift. Life must be lived. I will live mine.

You've always known that the movie *The Color Purple* had a powerful effect on me, Sweetheart, particularly the ending when the mother, Celie, is reunited with her children. I feel certain now that it is the feeling I will have when you and I meet again at the top of the mountain. I cried hard when I saw that union, Katie. It was long before you had died. I had a similar response to the ending of the movie E.T.

Elliot, the little boy who befriended the alien E.T., asked him to "Stay" but E.T. responded quickly, "Come." There was a long moment when it became clear that Eliot was not going to go with E.T. on the space ship. It was then when the wise E.T. slowly raised his long crooked finger, touched Elliot's forehead and said, slowly and lovingly, **"I'll...be...right...here."**

And so you are, Katie, right here in my mind, in my heart and in my soul every blessed minute of every blessed day. I loved your moments of glad grace, Katie, and I know you are working from the other side now. I believe that with all my heart.

I will love you forever,
Your Mom

Epilogue

When a great ship is in harbor and moored, it is safe.
But...that is not what great ships are built for.

~CLARISSA PINKOLA ESTES~

Katie was a great ship who loved being on life's high seas. She never played it safe and neither does her mother. Life goes forward. Katie taught me that, so I am living my life and I am moving forward in my life. I would like to share some things with you which have transpired since Katie's passing.

One event was that my father-in-law died in September of 2006. He was almost ninety. January, 2008, my beloved sister Eileen died suddenly. She was fifty-four. My sister was one of the sweetest people I have ever known but she was a tortured soul after Jenny's death. She loved her son Eric very much but the sadness over losing her daughter was just too much. Eileen was always proud of me. I wanted to hand her a copy of this book for she loved Katie and she loved me - it was not meant to be. So I say be at peace, dear sister. Kiss our Katie, Jenny, Mom and Dad and tell Grandpop I fed the parakeets and Grandmom that I picked up the apples in the backyard and she owes me a dime.

I am also very happy to share with you, dear Reader, that our grandson Connor is now a precocious, sensitive, eight year old in the third grade. He reads at the fifth grade level and has the wisdom of Gandhi. We are very close. During a summer vacation in 2002, when he was just two and a half, I heard him making "psst, psst" noises outside my bedroom. I opened the door, smiled and picked him up. "Should Grandmom take you to the beach?" Off we dashed to the water just 200 yards away.

As the sun glistened on the horizon, Connor dug in the sand. It was just days before that Dick instructed him in how to pray in sophisticated Buddha style: hands out wide, then back together again. Without any promoting about praying Connor suddenly burst into a prayer and dropped to his knees, "Om, om," he prayed, "Thank you God for the beach, the sand, the sunny day, for Daddy and Mommy and Grandmom and Grandpa and Ellie." He grew quiet for a minute so I interjected, "And Aunt

Katie." Abruptly Connor stood up, looked directly into my eyes and said, "I am not sick anymore." Then he picked up his shovel and went back to his digging.

My mouth dropped open and my heart beat fast as I tried to absorb this powerful message - that Katie was present in that moment. After I caught my breath I started crying then swooped Connor up and ran - giant steps - back to the house where Richard stood drinking his morning coffee. Falling over my words I sobbed and recounted the incident. "Mom, you're not making this up just to make me feel good, are you?" I told him that of course I wasn't. Then I saw Dick looking at me with that wonderful Dick smile on his face, that smile I fell in love with, that smile that expressed his belief in me.

I have frequently wondered if this moment with Connor was what Katie had alluded to that day when she looked into my eyes and told me that I didn't understand but one day I would. I think, dear Reader that it was, because each time I have retold this story - to anyone - I could not stop my tears. I truly believe that Katie wanted me to know that she was well and safe and when Connor said those words out loud it was as though his little lips voiced a thought that was not his, that Connor was a channel through which dear Katie spoke. I also felt she had chosen him to be an intuitive presence in my life and that he and I would continue to understand one another without the strain and fuss that so many relationships demand. It was an amazing moment in my life that I will always hold as close as I hold him.

Dick and I also have two granddaughters, Ella Catherine, a six year old, honey haired adorable blonde who reminds me of the wind. She could easily become President of the United States. I am wild about her. One summer overnight, when she was four, she remarked out of the blue (or was that out of the soul), that she knows her daddy had a sister named Katie. Now I am very quiet and riveted on her. "Yes," I told her, "he did have a sister named Katie." She responded,

"And she was sick."

"Yes," I responded, "Katie was sick."

"And the doctors did everything and everything to make her well, Grandmom." Well now, that was it for me, I'm gone, and I started crying. She leaned over and hugged me, and patted my hand, just like that. Oh, and did I mention her due date was July 10? That is Katie's anniversary date.

Then there is Gracen Jane, our beautiful three year old comedic blue-eyed imp of a grandchild who likes both eating and wearing her lasagna. When I walk into a room, she runs to me hollering, "Grandmom! Grandmom!" Recently, Gracen and I decided that girls can burp, too, not just boys. I hold her close like the miracle that she is, this delightful child who was born on Easter Sunday, the feast of The Resurrection. Who knows what other miracles of hope are in store for me, for Dick, with these precious conduits of love! And if it is in store for me, it is in store for you, too, dear Reader.

Katie Brant was an amazing woman. She embraced her love of life and her fate. Her journey was hard but blessed; it had great sadness and challenge but great glory too. Katie's pilgrimage taught me many things because Katie was my greatest teacher. God made her perfect then He brought her home.

In closing I would say tenderly to you that in this lifetime you will suffer many losses and when a loss stares you in the face you will have a decision to make. Who will you then be? Loss will ask you "How will you live your life now?" You really do have a choice and you really can make the choice to let your loss help you to grow. Look to the blessings that are still in your life. Grab a hold of your family, your friends, your favorite book and your gratitude. As each day passes you will know how strong you can be; how courageous you really are; and how much love you cannot wait to give away.

So my Friends, be the love. Be the light. Pray for Katie. Pray for me.

Love,
M.J.

With Thanks and Appreciation

Thank you to Connor, my handsome and charming grandson. Besides his heart of gold, he has restored my hope in this life, taught me how to play football, a better game of chess and numerous computer tricks! I love writing stories together and talking about our dreams. He is a genius and wise both intellectually and diplomatically speaking. It feels quite magical to be his Grandma and I love him.

Thank you to Ellie, my Ella Bell, for her ongoing enthusiasm for just about everything. Her ability to stand her own ground is a birthright that she claimed before the age of two; it is a quality that I applaud about her. Ellie is a born leader, full of charisma, intelligence and beauty. She will also forever and ever be my little monkey. I adore being her Grandmom Monkey and I love her.

Thank you to Gracen Jane for always making me laugh and for being so relaxed and unselfconscious. Her natural sense of self-confidence and compassion for people's feelings is tender and inborn. Her beautiful blue eyes and angelic face match her joyful spirit and her even disposition. She completed the family circle and I love her.

Thanks to the voice of the good God which kept me focused on this labor of love. Thanks to all of the mothers everywhere who inspire me. Thanks to Katie's doctors, nurses and health care providers who treated and comforted her: Jonathan Finlay, M.D. who loved Katie for ten years. To dear departed Fred Epstein, M.D. To Jeff Wisoff, M.D., who performed four of Katie's five surgeries. To Ira Dunkle, M.D., Sharon Gardner, M.D., James Johnson, M.D., Charles Sklar, M.D., Anna Janss, M.D., Ph.D., Regina I. Jakacki, M.D., Beverly Lang, M.D., Roger Packer, M.D., Bruce Himelstein, M.D., William Adamson, M.D., Jean Belasco, M.D., Mary McElwain-Petriccione, RN, MSN, CPNP, Patricia Danz, R.N., Margaret Rose, R.N., Cynthia Robertson, R.N., Dave Dellago, Pharm.D, Quincy Bray and the many others who cared when we needed support.

Thanks to special friends in the publishing world for kindness and encouragement: Caryn Karmatz-Rudy, Executive Editor with Warner Books, who read my first draft tied with a pink ribbon and said, "keep going." Heartfelt thanks to Larry Kirshbaum, former Chairman of Warner Trade Publishing turned literary agent and friend, who supported me, "M.J., just get it out!" To gifted editor, Sally Arteseros, for her help. To Denise Marcil, literary agent and to Helen Rees, literary agent, whose sensitivities and suggestions were invaluable at a painfully vulnerable time. Thanks to Deanna Pagano for her help and advice. To Nathan Linn for help with the book's beautiful cover.

Thanks to my colleagues and friends: Jungian Analyst

James Hollis, Ph.D. His wealth of knowledge and writing style are models that I aspire to attain. Heart-felt love and appreciation to dear friend and colleague, Lennie Roche Perrot, M.S., whose unwavering encouragement helped the book evolve to what it has become; to Frank and Kate Kirk; to Jungian analyst Linda Carter; to author friend Mary Rose Nuse; to executive coach and friend Pam Godwin; to author friends Wendy Steinberg and Paul Zeltzer, M.D. Thanks to Rose O'Rourke, RN, Delores and Joe Santoro, Steve Martino, Elizabeth Martin and Edward Murray whose deep faith gave me wings; to friend Richard Caruso, Ph.D., Ernst & Young's 2006 Overall Entrepreneur of the Year. Love to Gail Neale Higgins who has supported me since 1962 in absolutely everything. Love to friends Ray and MarySue Hansell, Tammy Brenn and Robin Carr, M.D. whose presence and encouragement offered hope when I didn't think I would ever laugh again. Thanks for support to sisters-in-law Trish England and Wendy Brant. Love for encouragement to cousins Tom, Sandy, John and Irene Hurley. Thanks to my loyal brother Frank Hurley. He knows how I love him and our sister Eileen who always wanted the best for us. Thanks to my mother for my faith and her sacrifices. Thanks to my father for making me feel cherished.

Gratitude for my many clients who told me that they kept my notes in their wallets - their affirming voices directed me to write in epistolary style. Thank you to the Sisters of Notre Dame de Namur, for years of prayers for Katie. To the Sisters of Mercy from St. John's School and Camden Catholic High School who taught me how to love God. Thanks to the Sisters of Mercy at McAuley Convent and Merion Mercy for rocking the heavens for my intentions.

Deep gratitude and love to my amazingly handsome husband, Dick. Never was there a better father than he. I would marry him again for that alone. In addition to many readings and constructive edits of the manuscript, his constant love has helped me to grow up and that alone is a miracle.

Thank you to my wonderful and creative son, Richard, who along with my beautiful daughter-in-law, Caroline, suggested that I add more psychological insight. Richard has made me laugh since the day he was born, designed my website and is the son that every mother prays for. I treasure and love him. Gratefulness to Caroline who stepped into our complicated family picture with her generous heart to help whenever needed. I am in awe at the many things she excels at, especially being a mother and running Katie's Kids for the Cure with Rich. She is a force for good and I love her.

Soulful thanks, gratitude and love to my amazing agent, Maureen O'Crean, MBA. Her visionary mind, fun-filled personality and soulful spirit make me feel like a million bucks. I feel the sacred in this relationship turned friendship which I respect and treasure. Her joyful, trusting temperament, business genius and editing skills have demonstrated an intellect I would have had to search the world over for had I not been led to her, in the most natural way, at the *Simple Abundance* Leadership Training in Los Angeles, California. Seems there was quite a mysterious plan percolating behind the veil in that "City of Angeles." Just by showing up, Maureen O'Crean makes wonderful things happen. I know she has God's ear, too, because I would not be here today, thanking her, if she did not.

Thanks to Jonathan Donahue Carr, Chairman of Simple Abundance, Inc. and Sarah's lovely husband. I had the pleasure to celebrate his marriage to Sarah in Sir Isaac Newton's original digs. Besides being "smashing fun" he has an abundance of charm and gaiety which makes everyone feel welcome in his presence. I thank him for generously taking care of the legalities of the book and allowing me, along with Sarah and Maureen, to focus on the creativities.

And lastly, I can only scratch the mere surface of the gratitude that is in my heart for dear and precious friend, Sarah Ban Breathnach. She is a woman whose exquisite soul, books and writings have touched the deepest part of me, and many others, for years. When she dedicated *Something More* to Katie, she wrote how Katie became her spiritual catalyst for creating the Simple Abundance Press. I remember how proud she was! It is sublimely beautiful to piece together now how invisible hands have since moved my book forward and right into the arms of this very same press! And as if this isn't synchronistic and miraculous enough, I am also speaking of a friendship which has grown to transcend the ordinary, because whether we are sharing our joy, our pain, our delight about hats and stilettos, or just riding around in a top down convertible like Isadora Duncan, scarves blowing in the wind, I lift a Bailey's high to heaven above to convey my gratitude and love to Sarah because by shepherding the book into print she gave me not only the most profound Christmas gift that I have ever received, but a deep meaning to my Katie's returning to God. For now I have the blessed opportunity to help other hearts and souls on their individual pilgrimages. Being able to turn my pain into something beneficial and way larger than myself is a prayer answered.

Years ago Sarah told me that I was blessed among women. Well she, Sarah Ban Breathnatch, has made it so.

~Bibliography~

Allende, Isabel. *Paula*. New York: Harper Perennial, 1994.

Andersen, Hans Christian. *Andersen's Fairy Tales*. New York: Grosset & Dunlap, 1981.

Ban Breathnach, Sarah. *Simple Abundance: A Daybook of Comfort and Joy*. New York: Warner Books, 1994.

Ban Breathnach, Sarah. *Something More: Excavating Your Authentic Self*. New York: Warner Books, 1998.

Ban Breathnach, Sarah. *The Simple Abundance Companion*. New York: Warner Books, 2000.

Bartlett's Familiar Quotations, Sixteenth Ed., Edited by Justin Kaplan. Boston: Little Brown & Company, 1992.

Bolen, Jean Shinoda. *Goddesses In Every Woman: A New Psychology of Women*. San Francisco: Harper & Row, 1984.

Boss, Pauline. *Ambiguous Loss, Learning to Live with Unresolved Grief*. Cambridge, Massachusetts: Harvard University Press, 1999.

Campbell, Joseph with Bill Moyers. *The Power of Myths*. New York: Doubleday, 1988.

Chopra, Deepak. *The Seven Spiritual Laws of Success: A Practical Guide to the Fulfillment of Your Dreams.* California: Amber-Allen Publisher, 1995.

Diagnostic Criteria from DSM-IV-TR. Washington, DC: American Psychiatric Association, 2000.

Estes, Clarissa Pinkola. *Women Who Run With The Wolves: Myths and Stories of the Wild Woman Archetype.* New York: Ballantine Books, 1992.

Eadie, Betty J. *Embraced by the Light.* California: Gold Leaf Press, 1992.

Frank, Anne. *Anne Frank: The Diary of a Young Girl.* New York: Pocket Books, 1953.

Gibran, Kahlil. *The Prophet.* New York: Alfred A. Knopf, 1988.

Gilbert, Roberta M. *Extraordinary Relationships: A New Way of Thinking About Human Interactions.* Minneapolis: Chromimed Publishing, 1992.

Hall, Calvin S. and Nordby, Vernon J. *A Primer of Jungian Psychology.* New York: A Mentor Book/Penguin Books USA Inc., 1973.

Hall, Calvin S. *A Primer of Freudian Psychology.* Ohio: The World Publishing Co., 1954.

Hillman, James. *The Soul's Code: In Search of Character and Calling.* New York: Random House, 1996.

Hollis, James. *The Middle Passage: From Misery to Meaning in Midlife.* Toronto: Inner City Books, 1993.

Hollis, James. *Finding Meaning in the Second Half of Life: How to Finally, Really Grow Up.* New York: Gotham Books, 2005.

Hollis, James. *Why Good People do Bad Things: Understanding Our Darker Selves.* Gotham Books, 2007.

Jung, C.G. *Collected Works of C.G.Jung.* Translated by R.F.C. Hull. Princeton: Princeton University Press, 1972.

Lewis, C.S. *A Grief Observed.* New York: HarperCollins Publishers, 2001 edition.

Lives of the Saints: Daily readings. Chicago: Franciscan Herald Press, 1983.

McCourt, Frank. *Angela's Ashes: A Memoir.* New York: Scribner, 1996.

Miller, Alice. For *Your Own Good: Hidden Cruelty in Child-rearing and the Roots of Violence.* New York: The Noonday Press, 1990.

Moore, Thomas. *Care of the Soul: A Guide for Cultivating Depth and Sacredness in Everyday Life.* New York: Harper Collins, 1992.

The New American Bible, Saint Joseph Edition. New York: Catholic Book Publishing Company, 1970.

The New Beacon Book of Quotations by Women, compiled by Rosalie Maggio. Boston:Beacon Press, 1996.

O'Donohue, John. *Anam Cara: A Book of Celtic Wisdom.* New York: Cliff Street Books/Harper Collins, 1997.

O'Donohue, John. *Eternal Echoes.* New York: Bantam Press, 1998.

Sanders, Catherine M. *How To Survive The Loss of a Child: Filling the Emptiness and Rebuilding Your Life.* Rochlin, CA: Prima Publishing, 1992.

Scarf, Maggie. *Intimate Worlds: Life Inside the Family.* New York: Random House, 1995.

Scarf, Maggie. *Secrets, Lies, Betrayals, The Body/Mind Connection: How the Body Holds the Secrets of a Life, and How to Unlock Them.*

New York: Random House, 2004.

Tan, Amy. *The Opposite of Fate – Memories of a Writing Life.* New York: Penguin Books, 2003.

A Treasury of Children's Literature. Edited by Armand Eisen. Boston: Houghton Mifflin Company, 1992.

Viorst, Judith. *Necessary Losses.* New York: Simon & Schuster, 1986.

Van Allsburg, Chris. *The Polar Express.* Boston: Houghton Mifflin Company, 1985.

Walker, Alice. *The Color Purple.* New York: Pocket Books, a Division of Simon & Schuster, Inc., 1982.

Whitmont, Edward C. and Perera, Sylvia Brinton. *Dreams, A Portal To The Source.* New York: Routeledge, 1989.

Yates, Jenny. *Jung on Death and Immortality.* New Jersey: Princeton University Press, 1999.

Yeats, William Butler. *Selected Poems of.* Edited by Stuart Miller. New York: Barnes & Noble Books, 1994.

M.J.'s Contact Page

Katie's Kids for the Cure (www.katieskids.org) will receive a portion of the proceeds from the sale of this book keeping with Katie's dream of cause-related marketing. Please look over the website if you would like to be a part of the team and donate to find a cure to rid children of brain tumors.

Please check out my website at www.MJHB.net or visit my blog on www.wheneverydaymatters.com to post your thoughts and feelings about *When Every Day Matters: A Mother's Memoir on Love, Loss and Life* and how it has touched your life. You can also contact me at the following address:

M. J. Hurley Brant

P. O. Box 188

Bryn Mawr, PA 19010-0188

maryjanebrant@gmail.com

Also, take a moment to look over Sarah's Ban Breathnach's website to become part of the Simple Abundance family www.simpleabundance.com

About the Author

Mary Jane Hurley Brant, M.S., C.G.P. is a certified group psychotherapist and a Certified Leader of Simple Abundance Seminars and Workshops. For twenty-eight years she has worked as a Human Relations Counselor with a concentration in Jungian studies and depth psychology. Throughout her long career, M.J. has worked with hundreds of individuals, couples, groups and in hospice to bring meaning to their lives. M.J. believes her spiritual calling is helping people define and meet their personal goals, be honest with themselves and others and discover their true and loving spirits for living an authentic life. She lives in PA with her husband and near her grandchildren.

Katie Brant

Beannacht
(Blessing)
By John O'Donohue

On the day when
The weight deadens
On your shoulders
And you stumble,
May the clay dance
To balance you.

And when your eyes
Freeze behind
The gray window
And the ghost of loss
Gets into you,
May a flock of colors,
Indigo, red, green
And azure blue,
Come to awaken in you
A meadow of delight.

When the canvas frays
In the curragh of thought
And a stain of ocean
Blackens beneath you,
May there come across the waters
A path of yellow moonlight
To bring you safely home.

Printed in the United States
205051BV00002B/103-315/P

9 780981 780900